BLUEPRINTS

History
Key Stage 1
Teacher's Resource Book

D0756487

Second Edition

Wendy Clemson

Stanley Thornes (Publishers) Ltd

Do you receive BLUEPRINTS NEWS?

Blueprints is an expanding series of practical teacher's ideas books and photocopiable resources for use in primary schools. Books are available for separate infant and junior age ranges for every core and foundation subject, as well as for an ever widening range of other primary teaching needs. These include **Blueprints Primary English** books and **Blueprints Resource Banks**. **Blueprints** are carefully structured around the demands of National Curriculum in England and Wales, but are used successfully by schools and teachers in Scotland, Northern Ireland and elsewhere.

Blueprints provide :

- *Total curriculum coverage*
- *Hundreds of practical ideas*
- *Books specifically for the age range you teach*
- *Flexible resources for the whole school or for individual teachers*
- *Excellent photocopiable sheets - ideal for assessment and children's work profiles*
- *Supreme value*

Books may be bought by credit card over the telephone and information obtained on **(0242) 228888**. Alternatively, photocopy and return this **FREEPOST** form to receive **Blueprints News**, our regular update on all new and existing titles. You may also like to add the name of a friend who would be interested in being on the mailing list.

Please add my name to the **BLUEPRINTS NEWS** mailing list.

Mr/Mrs/Miss/Ms --

Home address --

--Postcode -------------------------

School address --

-- Postcode -------------------------

Please also send **BLUEPRINTS NEWS** to :

Mr/Mrs/Miss/Ms --

Address --

-- Postcode -------------------------

To: Marketing Services Dept., Stanley Thornes Ltd, FREEPOST (GR 782), Cheltenham, GL50 1BR

First published in 1991 by:
Stanley Thornes (Publishers) Ltd
Ellenborough House
Wellington Street
CHELTENHAM GL50 1YD
England

Reprinted 1993
Reprinted 1994
2nd edition 1995

A catalogue record for this book is available from the British Library.

ISBN 0–7487–2208–4

Typeset by Tech-Set, Gateshead, Tyne & Wear.
Printed and bound in Great Britain at the Bath Press, Avon.

CONTENTS

ACKNOWLEDGEMENTS

Special thanks to Frances for her forbearance and William for dispassionately challenging what appeared in draft. Thanks also to Jill Doyle and Joan Taylor, the Northwich librarians who were unfailingly helpful in the face of near impossible requests.

HMSO for permission to reproduce extracts from History in the National Curriculum (1995).

INTRODUCTION

What is *Blueprints: History*?

Blueprints: History is a practical teachers' resource written to fulfil all the requirements of the National Curriculum in history (1995). Because of its structure, *Blueprints History Key Stage 1* can also be profitably used by teachers and schools not following National Curriculum courses and you will find links to the other UK curricula included in this edition. It is intended to be used flexibly, either as an ideas bank for individual teachers or as a workable core resource for a whole school's scheme of work in history.

Blueprints History consists of materials for Key Stages 1 and 2. For each stage, there is a Teacher's Resource Book and a book of Pupils' Copymasters. This Teacher's Resource Book provides hundreds of practical ideas and activities for 5 to 7 year olds and can be used on its own, as a freestanding resource, without the accompanying copymaster book. The book of Pupils' Copymasters provides 98 photocopiable worksheets linked to the many activities in this book. The worksheets reinforce and extend activities already done, and provide opportunities to build up a record of the children's work in history. They may also be seen as a resource for assessment.

Blueprints: History and the National Curriculum

Blueprints: History has been written to fulfil the requirements of the National Curriculum in history for primary schools. The resources for each Key Stage have been structured to cover the relevant programme of study.

This Key Stage has been written around common infant topics, an approach which allows you to integrate your history work into your cross-curricular planning and to fit history into a crowded timetable. It also matches well with the Key Stage 1 programme of study, which does not specify the content in great detail – unlike the programme of study at Key Stage 2. (For this reason *Blueprints: History Key Stage 2* is structured differently, around the core Study Units.) Together, the resources for the two Key Stages can be used as a continuous and coherent scheme for teaching history in the National Curriculum.

The topics at Key Stage 1 provide opportunities to cover the whole programme of study and the whole Attainment Target in a variety of ways. Each contains activities that will allow children to demonstrate learning at levels 1, 2 and 3. You can be confident that using just some of these topics will mean that you are meeting the requirements of Key Stage 1. You will find

a ready-reference guide to the National Curriculum in the next section, with examples of activities within the book which fulfil the requirements. Additionally, at the end of work relating to each topic there is a chart showing the suggested Level(s) of work involved in each activity, so that you can, if you wish, best fit children's work against the Level Indicators.

Topics at Key Stage 1

Besides being ideal for cross-curricular planning and meeting the requirements of the National Curriculum, the topic approach allows you the flexibility to follow lines of enquiry which interest the particular children you are teaching. You can work on a topic for a few days or several weeks, spending a few minutes a day on it or one session per day or per week. Topics are highly motivating and allow children to make connections between apparently disparate ideas in a meaningful way. Topic work in history gives the children opportunities to develop and practise those research skills which are important to being a historian, skills that are vital if they are to gain an understanding of the past.

The topics can be used in any order. Each begins with a topic web which sets out a summary of the aspects covered. Following this are suggestions about how to extend history into other curriculum areas, general points to be aware of in that particular topic, and some background historical information to help with your own planning. Then a section entitled *Resources* offers general suggestions about resourcing the topic.

In a separate section entitled *Skills for children*, beginning on page xx, you will find suggestions for activities designed to develop children's competence in research work, including specific examples from the topic work. This section addresses the key elements in the Programme of Study.

Within each topic there are core and extension activities. It is intended that the core activities should be seen as forming the work central to the topic. You can begin with any of the activities and proceed in any order, covering either some or all of the strands on the topic web.

The extension activities are intended for children whom you wish to proceed with their study beyond the core activities. However, the extension activities can, if you wish, form the basis for a whole new set of investigations and be used as new topic titles for part or all of the class. For example, one year you may choose to do a topic called 'Homes'; the next year you may begin with a topic called 'Gardens'.

Developing history skills

The section in this book entitled *Skills for children*, beginning on page xx, comprises activities and suggestions which specifically support children in acquiring essential study skills for their development as historians. They act as an adjunct to the book, for they are not 'topic specific'. The skills section addresses the Key Elements in the Programme of Study. This section offers ways in which you can help children to, for example, formulate and ask questions; make networks of ideas; and observe, discuss and experiment, in order to find and evaluate evidence and opinion. It also offers suggestions regarding the use of secondary sources like photographs, the written word and databases; and for helping children to make judgements about these and about how to communicate the results of their work in a variety of ways.

The skills activities and suggestions are especially useful in deciding 'where to start' with a class that is new to you, or with an additional entrant to the class, and in establishing which kinds of activities need more practice. They serve, therefore, as an important assessment tool for teachers, and as practice and self-appraisal activities for children. Individual children can record their own progress in acquiring skills on the self-appraisal sheet included on page 103 of this book. You are free to photocopy this page for use in school, and the same record sheet also appears on Copymaster 97 in the book of Pupils' Copymasters.

Links with other books in the Blueprints series

On page xv there are some suggested activities and sections found in other books in the Blueprints series which can augment the children's History topic work and link their work to other areas of the curriculum.

Record keeping

There is a child summary sheet on page 104 of this book, which you can use to log the topics worked on by each child and the Level(s) at which the child has worked. You are free to photocopy this page for use in school, and the same record sheet also appears on Copymaster 98 in the book of Pupils' Copymasters.

Using the copymasters

If you also have the book of Pupil Copymasters, use them to support learning and help with consolidation, assessment and evaluation. Each topic is accompanied by a number of copymasters (a total of 78 for all the topics) and there is also a section of more general skills-based copymasters at the end (Copymasters 79 to 96). The copymasters are fun to do and have been designed to be used by children with little help from the teacher. There are, however, conceptual leaps on some of them, which should be negotiated by you; for example, on Copymaster 7 the entrance to a castle cannot really be compared to that of a modern house, for the castle would have housed a community of people, comprising many families.

In this book the copymasters appropriate to a particular section are referred to by this symbol

which appears on the right-hand side of the section heading. There are also references in bold type within the individual activities to which the copymasters relate.

For reference purposes, the programme of study is set out below for Key Stage 1. Alongside each area of study and each key element you will find a list of activity and copymaster numbers. These have been included as examples of how activities and copymasters can be locked into the National Curriculum.

It is important to remember that, in order to meet the National Curriculum requirements, children need to engage in activities which establish starting points for historical study. For example, there must be some discussion of what life is like now. The activities, therefore, vary in how closely they map onto the programme of study.

Following this section are Attainment Target Level Descriptions and examples of activities which should allow children to demonstrate work at each Level. At the end of each topic you will find that the activities have been levelled to enable you to 'best fit' children's work against the Level Descriptions.

KEY STAGE 1 PROGRAMME OF STUDY

Pupils should be given opportunities to develop an awareness of the past and of the ways in which it was different from the present. They should be helped to set their study of the past in a chronological framework and to understand some of the ways in which we find out about the past.

The Areas of Study and the Key Elements, outlined below, should be taught together.

AREAS OF STUDY

■ **1.** Pupils should be taught about the everyday life, work, leisure and culture of men, women and children in the past, *eg clothes, diet, everyday objects, houses, shops and other buildings, jobs, transport, entertainment*. In progressing from familiar situations to those more distant in time and place, pupils should be given opportunities to investigate:

a changes in their own lives and those of their family or adults around them;

> Examples
> *Family:* Core Activities 8, 11, 14.
> *Being a child:* Core Activity 8.
> *Homes:* Core Activities 4, 5.

b aspects of the way of life of people in Britain in the past beyond living memory.

> Examples
> *Going to work:* Core Activity 7.
> *Money and shops:* Core Activity 9.

■ **2.** Pupils should be taught about the lives of different kinds of famous men and women, including personalities drawn from British history, *eg rulers, saints, artists, engineers, explorers, inventors, pioneers.*

> Examples
> See information about famous men and women on page xiii.
> *Seaside holidays:* Extension Activity 1.

■ **3.** Pupils should be taught about past events of different types, including events from the history of Britain, *eg notable local and national events, events in other countries, events that have been remembered and commemorated by succeeding generations, such as centenaries, religious festivals, anniversaries, the Gunpowder Plot, the Olympic Games.*

Examples
Celebrations: Core Activities 3, 4;
Extension Activity 2.
Copymaster 73.

KEY ELEMENTS

The Key Elements are closely related and should be developed through the Areas of Study, as appropriate. Not all the Key Elements need to be developed in each Area of Study.

Pupils should be taught:

■ **1. Chronology**

  a to sequence events and objects, in order to develop a sense of chronology;

Examples
Family: Core Activity 9.
Toys: Core Activity 9.
School: Core Activity 15.
Food and cooking: Core Activity 8.
Copymasters 43, 75.

  b to use common words and phrases relating to the passing of time, *eg old, new, before, after, long ago, days of the week, months, years.*

Examples
Seaside holidays: Core Activity 19.
School: Core Activity 15.
People and animals: Core Activity 10.
Copymaster 9.

■ **2. Range and depth of historical knowledge and understanding**

  a about aspects of the past through stories from different periods and cultures, including stories and eyewitness accounts of historical events;

Examples
Family: Core Activity 3, Extension Activity 2.
Homes: Core Activity 1.
Seaside holidays: Extension Activity 2.
Being a child: Core Activities 6 and 9.
People and animals: Core Activity 6.
Copymaster 33.

  b to recognise why people did things, why events happened and what happened as a result;

Examples
Family: Core Activity 11.
Seaside holidays: Core Activity 9.
Transport: Core Activities 11 and 12.

  c to identify differences between ways of life at different times.

Examples
Homes: Core Activity 17.
Clothes: Core Activity 15.
Being a child: Core Activity 9.
Copymasters 50, 61.

■ 3. Interpretations of history

a to identify different ways in which the past is represented, *eg pictures, written accounts, films, television programmes, plays, songs, reproductions of objects, museum displays.*

Examples
Clothes: Core Activities 12, 16.
Toys and games: Core Activity 18.
Copymaster 23.

■ 4. Historical enquiry

a how to find out about aspects of the past from a range of sources of information, including artefacts, pictures and photographs, adults talking about their own past, written sources, and buildings and sites;

Examples
Seaside holidays: Core Activity 21.
School: Core Activity 15.
People and animals: Core Activity 3.

b to ask and answer questions about the past.

Examples
School: Core Activity 12.
Going to work: Core Activity 13.
Money and shops: Extension Activity 2.

■ 5. Organisation and communication

a to communicate their awareness and understanding of history in a variety of ways.

Examples
Clothes: Core Activities 10, 16.
Toys and games: Core Activity 15.
Celebrations: Core Activity 14.
Food and cooking: Core Activity 17.
Transport: Core Activity 14.

Attainment Target

LEVEL DESCRIPTIONS

The following level descriptions describe the types and range of performance that pupils working at a particular level should characteristically demonstrate. In deciding on a pupil's level of attainment at the end of the key stage, teachers should judge which description best fits the pupil's performance. Each description should be considered in conjunction with the descriptions for adjacent levels.

By the end of Key Stage 1, the performance of the great majority of pupils should be within the range of Levels 1 to 3.

■ Level 1

Pupils recognise the distinction between present and past in their own and other people's lives. They show their emerging sense of chronology by sequencing a few events and objects, and by using everyday terms about the passing of time. They know and recount episodes from stories about the past. They are beginning to find answers to questions about the past from sources of information.

Examples
Family: Core Activity 3.
Clothes: Core Activity 3.
Toys: Core Activities 3, 4.
Going to work: Core Activities 5, 6.
Copymasters 18, 25, 34.

■ Level 2

Pupils show their developing sense of chronology by using terms concerned with the passing of time, by ordering events and objects, and by making distinctions between aspects of their own lives and past times. They demonstrate factual knowledge and understanding of aspects of the past beyond living memory, and of some of the main events and people they have studied. They are beginning to recognise that there are reasons why people in the past acted as they did. They are beginning to identify some of the different ways in which the past is represented. They answer questions about the past, from sources of information, on the basis of simple observations.

Examples
Money and shops: Core Activities 6, 9.
People and animals: Core Activity 10.
Transport: Core Activities 3, 5.
Food and cooking: Core Activities 11, 13.
Clothes: Core Activities 10, 16.
Copymasters 72, 75, 52, 10

■ Level 3

Pupils show their understanding of chronology by their increasing awareness that the past can be divided into different periods of time, their recognition of some of the similarities and differences between these periods, and their use of dates and terms. They demonstrate factual knowledge and understanding of some of the main events, people and changes drawn from the appropriate programme of study. They are beginning to give a few reasons for, and results of, the main events and changes. They identify some of the different ways in which the past is represented. They find answers to questions about the past by using sources of information in ways that go beyond simple observations.

Examples
Communication: Core Activity 12, Extension Activity 5
Being a child: Core Activity 9, Extension Activity 3
Food and cooking: Extension Activities 1, 2, 3
Copymasters 27, 28, 29, 45, 47, 65.

RESOURCES

In addition to artefacts, pictures, photographs, and information from a variety of sources, the following are important:

- A cumulative store of facts about the community of the school.
- Story and information books for children.
- Books for teachers.

There follow some suggestions about each of these.

Resources from the community

Here are some ideas for sources of information and subjects of interest:

- Local records, for example, church, library, town hall.
- Buildings of local importance, for example, the civic centre, hospital, almshouses.
- Buildings of historical importance because of their architectural style or who once lived there.

- People of local importance, for example, the mayor.
- Names of famous people who once lived locally.
- Names of local people with memories they are willing and able to share with young children.
- Names of local groups who may provide resources or a speaker for history topics, for example, local history and oral history societies, amateur dramatics societies, collectors of antiques of all kinds (e.g. postcards, toys, costumes, furniture).

BOOKS FOR CHILDREN

Story books
There is a book list within each topic. These include mainly contemporary stories rather than those set in the past, because there seem to be very few books with historical themes available for young children. However, even books about contemporary life can be starting points for discussions comparing the present day with how things used to be.

Information books
The information book list within each topic gives some titles to look out for. When the title is one of a series, you can check the usefulness of others in the same series. In addition, the children may find the following useful:

Amery, H. *Then and Now*, Usborne.
Brooks, F. and Edom, H. *The Usborne Book Of Living Long Ago*.
Gee, R. *Living in Castle Times*, Usborne First History Books.
Goodall, J. S. *An Edwardian Summer*, Macmillan.
Goodall, J. S. *Above and Below Stairs*, Macmillan.
Goodall, J. S. *The Story of an English Village*, Macmillan.
Patrick, G. *Family Life in World War II* from the series 'Beginning History', Wayland.
Thomson, N. *When I was young* and *World War II*, Franklin Watts.
Wagstaff, S. *Two Victorian Families*, A & C Black.

BOOKS FOR TEACHERS ▶

Poetry books

Here is a selection of titles within which poems related to the topics in this book can be found:

Ahlberg, A. *Heard it on the Playground*, Viking Kestrel.
Bennett, J. *People Poems*, Oxford University Press.
Cole, W. *Beastly Boys and Ghastly Girls*, Methuen Paperbacks.
Curry, J. *The Beaver Book of School Verse*.
Daniel, M. *A First Golden Treasury of Children's Verse*, (there is also a second book and both contain Victorian and Edwardian pictures of children), Macmillan Premier Picturemac.
Elson, D. *Cats Cats* (poems and prose), World's Work.
Foster, J. *A Very First Poetry Book*, Oxford University Press.
Graham, E. *A Puffin Book of Verse*.
Grindley, S. *Meet the Family*, Orchard Books.
Harrison, M. and Stuart-Clark, C. *The Oxford Book of Story Poems*, Oxford University Press.
Harvey, A. *Occasions: Everyday and Special Day Happenings*, Blackie.
Harvey, A. *Faces in a Crowd: Poems about People*, Viking Kestrel.
Harvey, A. *A Picnic of Poetry: Poems about Food and Drink*, Penguin.
McGough, R. *The Kingfisher Book of Comic Verse*, Kingfisher.
Magorian, M. *Waiting for my Shorts to Dry*, Viking Kestrel.
Rosen, M. *The Kingfisher Book of Children's Poetry*.
Stevenson, R. L. *A Child's Garden of Verses*, Macmillan.

Reference books

Anderson, J. and Swinglehurst, E. *The Victorian and Edwardian Seaside*, Country Life Books.
Battersby, J. and Tilley, D. *Modern Farming* from the series 'Finding out about', Franklin Watts.
Brooke-Little, J. P. *Boutell's Heraldry*, Frederick Warne.
Cribb, J. *Money* from the series 'Eyewitness Guides', Dorling Kindersley.
Davies, J. *The Victorian Kitchen*, BBC Books.
Davies, P. and Maile, B. *First Post: From Penny Black to the Present Day*, The Post Office/Quiller Press.
Dawes, F. V. *Not in Front of the Servants: A True Portrait of Upstairs, Downstairs Life*, Century Hutchinson.
De Haan, D. *Antique Household Gadgets*, Blandford Press.
Ellenby, J. *The Stuart Household* and *The Georgian Household*, Dinosaur Publications.
Ereira, A. *The People's England*, Routledge and Kegan Paul.
Fines, J. *Life in the Middle Ages*, Sampson Law.
Fry, P. S. *1000 Great People through the Ages*, Hamlyn.
Fry, P. S. *The Kings and Queens of England and Scotland*, Dorling Kindersley.
Grender, I. *An Old-Fashioned Christmas*, Hutchinson.

Harrison, J. F. C. *The Common People*, Fontana Press.
Harrison, M. *Growing Up in Victorian Days*, Wayland.
Huxley, A. *An Illustrated History of Gardening*, Paddington Press.
Kelsall, F. *How We Used to Live 1902–1926*, A & C Black.
Kerrod, R. *Encyclopaedia of the Animal World: Pets and Farm Animals*, Facts on File.
Lambert, M. *Twentieth-Century Transport* from the series 'The Twentieth Century', Wayland.
Lofts, N. *Domestic Life in England*, Weidenfield and Nicolson.
Loxton, H. *Guide to the Cats of the World*, Elsevier.
Marshall, P. *Railways*, Macdonald.
Mitchell, S. and Reeds, B. *Coins of England and the United Kingdom*, Seaby.
Moncrief, M. C. S. *Kings and Queens of England*, Blandford Press.
Moncrieffe, I. and Pottinger, D. *Simple Heraldry Cheerfully Illustrated*, John Bartholomew and Son.
Pinnell, Miss. (with the help of the children of Sapperton School) *Village Heritage*, Alan Sutton.
Pinnell, Miss. *Village Camera*, Alan Sutton.
Purton, R. W. *Churches and Religions*, Blandford Press.
Quennell, M. and C. H. B. *A History of Everyday Things in England, Volume III 1851–1914*, Batsford.
Reaney, P. H. *A Dictionary of British Surnames*, Routledge and Kegan Paul.
Rosen, M. *Autumn Festivals* and others in the series 'Seasonal Festivals', Wayland.
Ruby, J. *The 1920s and 1930s* from the series 'Costume in Context', Batsford.
Suares, J. and Chwast, S. *The Illustrated Cat*, Push-pin Press/Harmony.
Trease, G. *Timechanges: The Evolution of Everyday Life*, Kingfisher Books.
Unicef, *For Every Child: Celebrating the 30th anniversary of the Universal Declaration of the Rights of the Child*, Hutchinson.
Unstead, R. J. *Kings, Barons and Serfs: A Pictorial History 1086–1300* and *Years of the Sword: A Pictorial History 1300–1485*. These are examples from Unstead's series 'A History of the English speaking World', Macdonald.
Whone, H. *Church, Monastery, Cathedral: An Illustrated Guide to Christian Symbolism*, Element Books.
Wilkins, F. *Growing up between the Wars*, Batsford.

Books for fun

Snell, G. *Hysterically Historical: Madcap Rhymes of Olden Times*, Arrow Books.
Wood, T. *Horrible History*, Simon and Schuster.
The series 'Great Tales from Long Ago', for example, *Dick Whittington, Robin Hood* and *King Arthur's Sword* by C. Storr, Methuen.

INFORMATION ABOUT FAMOUS MEN AND WOMEN ▶

There are four important points to bear in mind when making decisions about whether to draw children's attention to a famous person in history. They are these:

● There are problems in choosing who to study because opinions vary about who should feature in a list of the famous in history.

● Those people chosen for study may act as role-models for today's children. If you give class time to warriors rather than philanthropists, and to industrialists rather than artists, the effects on the children's judgement about what most influences people's lives may be profound. Also, the idea that only men can be inspirational or influential is no longer an acceptable message to give to girls or boys.

● Historical insight is culturally determined; those featuring prominently in our history books may not even get a mention in books produced in other nations. Later in this section there is a starter list of names of people to study – most are British and so it is in no way a comprehensive or even representative list of all those people that a child should know about.

● Though, to some extent, we must take account of people's personalities and life circumstances in assessing their contribution to society, these factors can be given less importance by viewing them on a timeline. For example, I would prefer to see Florence Nightingale's contribution as a part of change in health care through the ages, rather than as an embodiment of virtues desirable in women and/or nurses. But, to complete the time-line, the children would really need to know a little about modern developments, and the more contemporary the people we study, the more contentious is an estimate of their contribution.

Despite the problems involved, you will still need to choose whose life or work the children should study. The names suggested on page xvi have been chosen with these criteria in mind:

— They are relatively easily researched.
— Something about the work they did, and some-times their personal lives, is within the under-standing of small children.

Kings and Queens of England (1066–present)

House of Normandy
William I (1066–87)
William II (Rufus) (1087–1100)
Henry I (1100–35)
Stephen (1135–54)

House of Plantagenet
Henry II (1154–89)
Richard I (the Lionheart) (1189–99)
John (1199–1216)
Henry III (1216–72)
Edward I (1272–1307)
Edward II (1307–27)
Edward III (1327–77)
Richard II (1377–99)

House of Lancaster (Plantagenet)
Henry IV (1399–1413)
Henry V (1413–22)
Henry VI (1422–61)

House of York (Plantagenet)
Edward IV (1461–83)
Edward V (1483)
Richard III (1483–85)

House of Tudor
Henry VII (1485–1509)
Henry VIII (1509–47)
Edward VI (1547–53)

Mary I (1553–58)
Elizabeth I (1558–1603)

House of Stuart
James I (1603–25)
Charles I (1625–49)

[No monarch 1649–60
Oliver Cromwell (1653–58) (Lord Protector)
Richard Cromwell (1658–60)]

Charles II (1660–85)
James II (1685–88)
Mary II (1688–94) and William III (1688–1702)
Anne (1702–14)

House of Hanover
George I (1714–27)
George II (1727–60)
George III (1760–1820)
George IV (1820–30)
William IV (1830–37)
Victoria (1837–1901)

House of Saxe-Coburg (Windsor from 1917)
Edward VII (1901–10)
George V (1910–36)
Edward VIII (1936)
George VI (1936–52)
Elizabeth II (1952–   )

The periods of British history

The periods of British history are labelled as follows;
The Middle Ages: there is a variety of dates given to
this period of history, one is from 5th Century A.D. to
The Battle of Bosworth in 1485, and 'medieval' means
pertaining to or in the style of The Middle Ages.
Subsequent periods are self-explanatory: Tudor, Stuart,
Georgian, Victorian, Edwardian. The dates of these can be
established from the chart of Kings and Queens.

Other famous people

Below are the names of other people whom you might
choose to study.

Homes, architecture, interior design
Laura Ashley
Thomas Chippendale
William Morris
Christopher Wren

Communication and literature (prose and poetry)
William Caxton
Sir Rowland Hill

John Evelyn
Samuel Pepys

Jane Austen
The Bronte Sisters
Lewis Carroll
Charles Dickens
Arthur Conan Doyle
William Shakespeare
Anthony Trollope

William Blake
Robert Browning
John Keats
Edward Lear
Alfred Tennyson
William Wordsworth

Industrial innovation and reform
Isambard K. Brunel
James Hargreaves
John L. Macadam
George Stephenson
Thomas Telford
'Turnip' Townshend

Those who worked for children
Robert Baden-Powell
Thomas Barnado

Medicine, health care and science
James L. Baird
Alexander Graham Bell
Charles Darwin
Michael Faraday
Alexander Fleming
William Harvey
Edward Jenner
Isaac Newton
Florence Nightingale

Soldiers, sailors, adventurers, explorers
James Cook
Francis Drake
Mary Kingsley
David Livingstone
Horatio Nelson
Walter Raleigh
Henry M. Stanley
Robert F. Scott
Arthur Wellesley (Duke of Wellington)

Music and art
Benjamin Britten
Charles Chaplin
John Constable
Edward Elgar
David Garrick
George Frederick Handel
Nellie Melba
Henry Moore
William Gilbert and Arthur Sullivan
Joseph M. W. Turner

Statesmen and social reformers
Elizabeth Fry
Winston Churchill
Emmeline Pankhurst
Robert Peel
Anthony Ashley Cooper (Lord Shaftesbury)
William Wilberforce

Others – famous and infamous
Mrs Beeton
Oliver Cromwell
Guy Fawkes
Mary Queen of Scots

Those who are famous but may not have existed
King Arthur
St George
Robin Hood

You will find that the history work in this book can be supported by a huge bank of related cross-curricular activities and copymasters across the whole **Blueprints** range of infant and Key Stage 1 books. The index below references related books which you may already have or may wish to acquire. Because of the number of references we have mainly given page and copymaster numbers only; however, where a particular book contains a substantial bank of related material the reference is given in *italics*. The following books were revised in 1995 to match the revised National Curriculum and all references for these books refer to the 1995 editions: *Blueprints Maths, Science, English, History, Geography, Maths Investigations, Science Investigations*. A detailed index of all the cross-references and links in the **Blueprints** series will be found in the *Blueprints Infant Topic Planner* (ISBN 0 7487 1748 X).

All topics
Maths KS1: Handling Data, all activities under this part of the programme of study can be done using historical data (*Copymasters 60–69*).

Family
Assemblies: *pp 39–47 family assembly;* **Art KS1:** Teacher's *pp 1–9 family topic*, Copymasters *1–10;* **Health Education KS1:** Teacher's *pp 23–32 family topic*, Copymasters *21–32;* **Maths Investigations:** copymaster – All about us; **Science Investigations:** Copymaster 14.

Homes
Art KS1: Teacher's *pp 10–19 homes topic*, Copymasters *11–42;* **Christmas KS1:** pp 41–49 photocopiable play 'Home'; **Geography KS1:** Teacher's (see the topic planner), Copymasters 34, 69, *75–82;* **Infant Geography Resource Bank:** *homes section copymasters 1–10* (see also topic index); **Infant Teacher's Resource Bank:** Copymasters 115–116, 126, 128, 133; **Science KS1:** Copymasters 44, 50–52; **Second Topics KS1:** *topic on buildings pp 39–55, topic on where we live pp 74–91;* **Technology KS1:** *pp 58–67 on houses*, see also the topic planner; **Topics 5–8:** *pp 63–76 complete homes topic;* **Writing 5–8:** Copymasters 3, 5, 8, 24, 31–34, 37, 46, 49, 51, 55.

Communication
Assemblies: pp 49–58 photocopiable assembly on signs and signals; **Art KS1:** Teacher's pp 63–70 topic on colour; **Geography KS1:** Teacher's (see topic planner on journeys), Copymasters 14, 22–23, 60, *93–102;* **Infant Geography Resource Bank:** *topic on moving around Copymasters 75–81;* **Science KS1:** Copymasters 2–7;

Second KS1 Topics: *topic on communication pp 110–133;* **Technology KS1:** *(see the topic planner for activities);* **Writing 5–8:** Copymasters 12, 42–45, 49, 59, 60, 63–70.

Clothes
Assemblies: pp 77–86 photocopiable assembly; **Art KS1:** Teacher's *pp 20–27 clothes topic*, Copymasters *43–50;* **Christmas KS1:** *pp 110–127 complete clothes topic;* **Geography KS1:** Copymasters 108–110; **Health Education KS1:** Copymasters 14, 68; **Infant Geography Resource Bank:** Copymasters 45–48; **Infant Teacher's Resource Bank:** Copymaster 129; **Religious Education KS1:** Copymasters 32, 45–49; **Science Investigations:** Copymasters 32, 37; **Science KS1:** Copymasters 75–76; **Technology KS1:** *see topic planner for activities;* **Topics 5–8:** *clothes topic pp 77–90;* **Writing 5–8:** Copymasters 1, 7, 11, 15–17, 19, 25, 26, 31, 39, 40, 44–46, 56, 57.

Toys and games
Art KS1: Teacher's (see topic index for activities), Copymasters 66, 94–95; **Christmas KS1:** pp 14–15 Christmas games; **Geography KS1:** Copymaster 103; **Maths Investigations:** Copymaster – counting songs and rhymes; **Science Investigations:** Copymaster 45; **Technology KS1:** *pp 16–26 on moving toys, pp 83–89 on directional games* (see also the topic planner); **Topics KS1:** *pp 1–21 toys topic.*

Seaside holidays
Assemblies: *pp 29–38 photocopiable summer assembly;* **Art KS1:** Teacher's pp 28–37 topic on water, Copymasters 51–56; **Distant Places:** topic on Corfu; **Environmental Education KS1:** pp 145–160 topic on oceans; **Geography KS1:** Copymaster 102; **Health Education KS1:** Copymasters 69, 84; **Infant Geography Resource Bank:** *topic on seaside villages 11–15*, 2, 83; **Science Investigations:** Copymaster 37; **Science KS1:** Copymaster 84; **Second KS1 Topics:** pp 92–109 topic on the sea; **Technology KS1:** *pp 75–82 on holidays* (see also topic planner); **Topics 5–8:** pp 47–62 topic on water; **The Writing Book:** Copymasters 71–74; **Writing 5–8:** Copymasters 19, 51, 58.

School
Geography KS1: Teacher's activities 13–15, 118, 138, 163, 171, 226, Copymasters 5, 70–71, 96; **Health Education KS1:** Copymaster 41; **Religious Education KS1:** Copymasters 65, 83; **Second KS1 Topics:** Where we live 3; **Technology KS1:** *pp 50–56 on the playground, pp 29–37 on classroom changes*, (see also the topic planner); **Topics KS1:** *pp 44–62 school topic;* **The Writing Book:** Copymasters 2, 7, 15, 30, 40, 52, 55, 60, 61, 63, 95; **Writing 5–8:** Copymasters 4–6.

Being a child

Health Education KS1: Teacher's *pp 13–22 topic on growing up,* Copymasters 11–32; **Religious Education KS1:** Teacher's *topic on Big Me and Little Me,* Copymasters *1–12, 17–18, 116–119;* **Science KS1:** Copymasters 9, *26–30,* 32; **Topics 5–8:** pp 1–16 *topic on myself;* **Topics KS1:** pp 97–119 *topic on my body;* **The Writing Book:** Copymasters 7, 41, 71–75; **Writing 5–8:** Copymasters 1–5, 8, 12–15, 21, 40.

Food and cooking

Assemblies: *pp 100–109 food assembly;* **Art KS1:** Teacher's *(see topic index);* **Christmas KS1:** *pp 128–141 topic on Christmas food;* **Environmental Education KS1:** *pp 94–110 food topic;* **Geography KS1:** Copymaster 46; **Infant Geography Resource Bank:** *Copymasters 41–44, 49–56;* **Infant Teacher's Resource Bank:** Copymasters 106–107; **Science Investigations:** Copymasters 4, 7, 21; **Science KS1:** Copymasters 21–23, 40; **Second KS1 Topics:** *pp 56–73 food and farming topic;* **Technology KS1:** (see topic planner); **The Writing Book:** Copymasters 71–72, 74; **Writing 5–8:** Copymasters 1, 9, 11, 13, 19, 25–30, 33, 37, 60, 70.

Transport

Art KS1: Teacher's *pp 47–53 complete transport topic,* Copymasters *63–68;* **Geography KS1;** Teacher's *(see topic planner on journeys),* Copymasters 23–24, 41, *93–102;* **Health Education KS1:** Copymasters 40–41; **Infant Geography Resource Bank:** Copymasters 72, 74, *topic on moving around 75–81,* 88, 97–102; **Infant Teacher's Resource Bank:** Copymaster 127: **Science Investigations:** Copymasters 61, 74; **Science KS1:** Copymasters 55–57, 64; **Second KS1 Topics:** the sea 6; **Technology KS1:** *pp 5–15 on vehicles* (see also topic planner); **Topics 5–8:** *pp 91–106 transport topic;* **Writing 5–8:** Copymasters 9, 10, 42–46, 50, 51, 54, 61, 62.

Going to work

Environmental Education KS1: *pp 128–144 topic on work;* **Geography KS1:** Teacher's *(see topic planner on jobs),* Copymasters *86–92;* **Infant Teacher's Resource Book:** Copymasters 121–122; **Religious Education KS1:** Copymaster 44; **Second Topics KS1:** *pp 20–38 topic on people who help us.*

People and animals

Art KS1: Teacher's pp 54–62 topic on living things, Copymasters 51–54, 57–59, 97; **Infant Geography Resource Bank:** Copymasters 41–47, 85, 87, 97–102; **Infant Teacher's Resource Bank:** 109–114, 117–118, 133, 136; **Science Investigations:** Copymasters 22–24; **Science KS1:** Copymasters 10, 34–35; **Seasonal Topics:** many activities throughout the book; **Technology KS1:** *pp 45–49 on pets (see also topic planner);* **Topics 5–8:** *pp 17–32 topic on pets;* **The Writing Book:** Copymasters 7, 10, 18, 29, 38, 49, 59, 79, 90; **Writing 5–8:** Copymasters 13, 37, 47.

Money and shops

Geography KS1: Teacher's *(see topic planner on shops),* Copymasters 7, 9, 40; **Infant Geography Resource Bank:** Copymasters 1, 4, 7, 37, 45, 52; **Maths Activities Resource Bank:** Copymasters 1–54; **Maths Investigations:** Copymaster – Counts; **Maths KS1:** Copymasters *9–12, 18, 20–23, 25–26, 34, 40, 50, 96;* **Technology KS1:** *(see topic planner).*

Celebrations

Art KS1: Teachers's pp 39–46 topic on circuses and fairs; **Christmas KS1:** *complete Christmas resource;* **Easter:** *complete Easter resource;* **Festivals:** *covers all major festivals;* **Infant Teacher's Resource Bank:** Copymasters 100–103; **Religious Education KS1:** Teacher's pp 15–25 *topic on birth celebrations,* Copymasters *11–20.*

Counting and measuring

Health Education KS1: Copymasters 15–16; **Infant Teacher's Resource Bank:** *Copymasters 1–13;* **Maths Activities Resource Bank:** *a large number of counting activities;* **Maths Investigations:** Copymasters – Measures and Measures 2; **Maths KS1:** *a very large bank of activities including copymasters 2–6, 9–14, 24, 29, 31, 36–39, 76–78, 84, 86–88, 92–101;*
Number Activities Resource Bank: *a large number of counting activities;* **Science Investigations:** Copymasters 66, 68; **Technology KS1:** (see the topic planner).

COVERAGE OF THE CURRICULUM FOR SCOTLAND, WALES AND NORTHERN IRELAND

Blueprints History Key Stage 1 covers nearly all the different history curriculum requirements in place for 5–7 year olds in Wales, Scotland and Northern Ireland. The activities in this book adopt a topic-based approach and develop historical skills and knowledge through the experience of children. They are therefore common to the first historical experiences of all children and are frequently 'content-free' or can easily be adapted to regional needs.

We have set out the key curriculum content for the relevant stages for Northern Ireland and Scotland with illustrative examples of activities and copymasters to demonstrate how activities in the book can be locked into these curricula.

As the wording of the National Curriculum for history for Wales at Key Stage 1 is almost identical to that of England, we would ask Welsh readers to refer to the guide on pages vii–x.

THE NATIONAL CURRICULUM FOR NORTHERN IRELAND

Key Stage 1
HSU: Core 1

Title: AN INTRODUCTION TO HISTORY

Focus and Structure

A planned structure of activities should be designed to relate to the intellectual development of the pupil and to develop the pupil's understanding of his/her own life within the wider context of time and his/her ability to sequence events, stories of artefacts in relation to each other. The HSU will focus on:

- pupils' own histories:

  Examples
  Being a child: Core Activity 1.
  Family: Core Activity 1;
  Copymaster 1.
  Transport: Core Activities 2 and 4.

- events in pupils' lives and in the lives of the adults around them:

  Examples
  Family: Core Activity 11;
  Extension Activity 2.
  Being a child: Core Activities 1–5.
  Food and cooking: Core Activities 6 and 7.

- stories about the past which help the pupils to distinguish between fantasy and reality:

  Examples
  School: Core Activity 13.

- local studies:

> **Examples**
> *Homes:* Core Activities 3–5
> *Money and shops:* Core Activities 7–10;
> Copymaster C67.

- traditional celebrations and ceremonies, local, national and worldwide, and how they contribute to an understanding of history:

> **Examples**
> *Family:* Extension Activities 1–2.
> *Celebrations:* Core Activities 1–14;
> Copymaster 70–73.

- use of artefacts and visual material to study the past:

> **Examples**
> *School:* Core Activity 15.
> *Seaside holidays:* Core Activities 7–15.
> *Family:* Extension Activity 2.

- conventions and vocabulary of time:

> **Examples**
> *Family:* Core Activities 6–7 and 9.

SCOTTISH NATIONAL GUIDELINES

SOCIAL SUBJECTS: Understanding People in the Past
Contexts and content for developing understanding

STAGES P1 to P2

In these first years, the emphasis should be on developing in pupils a sense of the past, mainly through using their own experience and their immediate environment and its past, and through stories about the past.

Studies should involve:
Studying people, events and societies of significance in the past

- the pupils' own past and the past of their families and communities, emphasising memories and the significant events

> **Examples**
> *Family:* Extension Activity 2;
> Copymaster 1.
> *Being a child:* Core Activities 4 and 5;
> Copymasters 38 and 39.
> *Seaside holidays:* Core Activities 5 and 6.

- stories which develop an awareness of the past:

> **Examples**
> *Being a child:* Core Activity 6.
> *Family:* Core Activity 3.
> *Communication:* Core Activity 3.

Developing an understanding of change and continuity, cause and effect:

■ changes affecting their own and other people's lives and the life of their community:

Examples
Family: Core Activities 8, 11
Homes: Core Activity 5.

■ simple cause and effect sequences in their own lives:

Examples
Homes: Core Activity 18.

Developing an understanding of time and historical sequence:

■ annual patterns and the sequence of events in their own and others' lives:

Examples
Family: Core Activities 5, 6.

■ ways of describing and measuring time:

Examples
Family: Core Activities 8, 9
Counting and measuring: Core Activity 6.

■ simple sequencing of historical items, eg objects, pictures

Examples
Clothes: Core Activity 11;
Copymaster 19.
Seaside holidays: Core Activity 11;
Copymaster 27.

Developing an understanding of the nature of historical evidence:

■ selected sources of historical evidence, particularly atefacts and visual sources:

Examples
Seaside holidays: Core Activities 7, 15.
School: Core Activity 15.
Toys and games: Extension Activity 2.

Considering the meaning of heritage

■ memories and memorabilia and their importance to families and communities:

Examples
Toys and games: Core Activities 3, 4
Family: Extension Activity 2.
Seaside holidays: Core Activity 10.

SKILLS FOR CHILDREN

While studying history, children can learn research skills that will be useful to them in all the subjects in the curriculum. Broadly speaking, these skills fall into three phases: collecting information, sorting out information and communicating outcomes. For historians, the emphasis is on the middle phase, for the evidence accumulated has to undergo rigorous scrutiny to establish its authenticity. I shall take each of the three phases of research in turn, and set out a number of activities which will help to develop children's competence. Also included are a number of examples taken from the topics within the book, which demonstrates how children are being given historical skills experience.

There are 'special' words used by historians, just as there is jargon attached to other subjects, and children need to know some of the language historians use before they can become skilled in historical investigation. For example, you will need to tell them what history is; the words we use for time past; the significance of dates and what a 'date' is; what a 'period' in history is and how the various periods are defined; what 'authentic' means and what constitutes 'evidence'. An understanding of all these things will not come before children 'do' history and practise history skills, but learning the jargon is an important part of that understanding.

COLLECTING INFORMATION ▶

Deciding what to do

Identifying the problem Explain to the children the difference between a specific and a general question. 'What did you have to eat for supper on Sunday?' is a specific question; 'What sort of things do you eat at suppertime?' is a more general one. See if the children can identify and generate specific and general questions – this will help them in refining problems.

Idea webs Show the children how to put a single problem or theme word (or picture) in the middle of a piece of paper and write or draw a number of ideas that spring from it. (See, for example, *Seaside holidays* Core Activity 2.)

Copymaster 79 provides a blank web that the children can fill with words or pictures.

Artefacts

Observation Talk to the children about *really* looking, and give them practice by setting up specific tasks with clues to identify. Play observation games; for example, put a number of objects on a tray, let the children see them for a few seconds, and then ask questions about the objects (now out of sight). Show the children how to use various magnifiers properly. Let them examine an historic artefact with the naked eye, say what they see, and then look through the magnifier and discuss any further evidence. (See, for example, *Family* Core Activity 10.)

Copymaster 80 is a record sheet for observations.

Discussion Talk to the children about the importance of sharing information and opinions, of listening and talking. During group work, give one group of children an artefact to pass around and talk about. Let them each have a chance to speak by allowing them to talk only when they are holding the object. When a child has made his or her observations, the object and the right to speak are passed on to the next child. Afterwards talk about what they learned from what others said. With practice, you should be able to leave the group for a couple of minutes while the interchange of opinions goes on. Let the children bring things from their own pasts and share them with the group. Help the children to manage listening and speaking when they have an 'expert' in their midst who is not an adult (in this case, the child who has brought something to show). (See, for example, *Clothes* Core Activity 16.)

Experiment Let the children try out some items from the past, for example, an old washboard, quill pens or a hand loom. Talk about the feelings involved in actually trying to do things as they were done long ago. Sometimes the children themselves could suggest how items might have been used and try out their ideas. (See, for example, *Food and cooking* Core Activity 11.)

People

Asking questions Let the children practise asking short questions (concerned with only one idea) and then listening and noting the answers to report orally to the other children. At first, you will need to phrase the questions, let the children do the asking, and then help them to report the replies. With practice, however, the children should begin to work out the wording for questions, so that they ask exactly what they want to know. For example, they could ask the head teacher what he or she did at age six, before going to school in the morning. When they are better able to formulate questions, they could ask the dinner lady something about her grandparents. (See, for example, *Toys and games* Core Activity 4.)

Questionnaires These are sophisticated research tools, and even experienced researchers find them difficult to construct. Help a group of children to work together in deciding what it is they want to find out from someone, and the form of words they wish to use. Keep the questions short, direct and simple. Let the children practise writing down one or two questions every time they are going to talk to someone about the past. Even if a questionnaire is not the final outcome, the writing of questions will help the children to think clearly about what they want to ask, and this will help them when they do come to the point where they can devise questionnaires. (See, for example, *School Extension Activity 4.*)

Copymaster 81 is a record sheet on which children can write their questions.

Pictures and photographs
Looking for evidence Show a small group a postcard or picture from the past with several people in it. Ask some deliberately leading questions, like:

How do you know the people are related?
What signs are there that the people are wealthy/not very well off?

On another occasion, and with a fresh picture, ask more open questions, like these:

What can you say about the people in this picture?
Where do you think the picture was taken?

Do you think this family is well off or poor? Why do you say that?
How do you think the people feel about having their picture taken?
How did people get a picture of their family before there were cameras?
What do you think the people in the picture did after their picture was taken?

On subsequent occasions, allow the children to pose questions for one another, using picture resources. (See, for example, *Seaside holidays* Core Activity 7.)

Copymasters 82 and 83 offer two pictures for the children to inspect and pose questions about.

Books and writing
Kinds of book Tell the children about fiction and non-fiction, and show them the 'parts' in both kinds of book. For example, they need to know what the 'Contents' is, how they can find out when the book was published, and how an index is arranged.

Library skills Give the children practice in looking things up. Make it easy at first by telling them what to look for on which page of which book. Then identify the book but not the page; and finally just set the problem and let the children do the book search themselves. Then show them where history books are kept in the school and public library and let them find the books they need in the former (they will still need your help in public libraries).

Copymaster 84 presents children with a quiz about library skills. The record-keeping exercise at the bottom can be continued on the back of the sheet.

TV and databases
Accessing information Show the children what a database is and let them practise getting information from a small database that you have set up, related to work they are doing. Then the children should put information they have collected into a database. (See, for example, *Family* Core Activity 14.)

SORTING INFORMATION ▶

Looking for clues
Present the children with pictures of groups, families and individual people and invite them to say what they consider important points about the people, giving the reasons for their judgements. The pictures should span several decades and generations.

Copymasters 85–91 provide pictures within which children can circle important clues and features, or the pictures can be used as material for oral discussion.

Copymaster 85 (top) shows a street scene in a Roman town in Britain, with a population of Roman soldiers and their households and the subjugated Britons. The bottom picture features a Saxon thane and his lady against a background of a Briton family at work on a farm.

Copymaster 86 (top) depicts a game of medieval football. The wealthy merchant on the left would have disapproved of the young apprentice boys 'wasting time' in this way when they should have been working. Below, wandering players entertain rich and poor in an inn-yard. These yards were the first theatres.

Copymaster 87 shows a city street scene in Stuart times; and a rural scene in early Georgian England. It was during the early part of the Georgian period that enclosures acts and new methods of farming forced agricultural workers deeper into poverty, while land-owners prospered.

Copymaster 88 shows the two faces of the Industrial Revolution, and **Copymaster 89** the two faces of Victorian urban society. Victorian slums, called rookeries, were tumbledown houses clustered in filthy alleys. Here dwelt some of the street workers – chimney-sweeps, dog-meat sellers, costermongers (who sold fruit and vegetables), rat-catchers, pedlars and wandering children (like the barefoot boy). In wealthy Victorian homes, musical evenings and tennis and croquet parties were favourite amusements. However, no games were permitted on Sundays, which were reserved for quiet family walks and bible readings. Everyone wore stiff, formal clothes.

Copymaster 90 illustrates the days of early motoring, at the beginning of the century. In those days the class system was still rigidly in place. But changes were on the way, as indicated in the lower picture, which shows women beginning to assert their rights. This new attitude, combined with the war years and the impact of new technology, was to revolutionise society in the space of a few decades.

Copymaster 91 shows some evidence of these changes. The top picture illustrates the mid-fifties days of skiffle parties and teddy-boys; and the bottom picture illustrates a street scene today.

Finding the important 'bits'

Read a short passage from a story (it need not be an historical story) and ask the children what were the three most important things in that part of the story. Opinions may differ, and you can discuss these differences. This is an activity that can be done repeatedly and it will help the children in all their studies. (See, for example, *School* Core Activities 5 and 6.)

Copymaster 92 is a challenge for children who have had some practice at making decisions about what is important information.

'True or false' and bias

Collect several reports about the same event. It may be that, with your help, the children can record older juniors' accounts of a school trip, or sports day, or a film they have seen in school. If you cannot collect this kind of information, use secondary resources, like newspaper accounts of a local event. Read them to the children and, with their help, decide on the emphasis (that is, the important points) in each account. Look for differences and talk about why these may have occurred – and what this means for the work of historians. (See, for example, *School* Extension Activity 3 and *Being a child* Core Activity 3.)

Look at a variety of historical objects and pictures, and discuss the importance of them being acknowledged as fitting a particular time. Talk about what forgeries, fakes, and reproductions are.

Copymasters 93–6 are pictures set in time, with some incongruities in them. Let the children spot as many as they can. Help them to find them all, for this work is not self-correcting.

On **Copymaster 93** the top picture depicts a medieval farm. The combine-harvester, aeroplane, electricity pylon and TV aerial on the dwelling are out of place. Below, in the picture of the Stuart inn, the post-box, van, can of coke and packet of crisps do not belong.

Copymaster 94 illustrates part of a large Tudor house, such as might have been owned by a very wealthy merchant. The poor in Tudor times lived in hovels – like the poor in almost every other age. The incongruities in the picture are the electric standard lamp and TV.

Copymaster 95 shows a well-off Georgian family at breakfast. In Georgian times there were no packets of cereals, processed fruit yoghurts, cartons of orange juice or tins of fruit.

The Edwardian ladies' clothes shop on **Copymaster 96** would not have included the jog-suit and trainers or the bikini amongst its wares. Credit cards are a comparatively recent invention, as is the skate-board.

LETTING OTHERS KNOW

Talking

Give the children chances to talk about their 'histoical findings' to a variety of audiences, including another child, a group, the class, the school, an adult in school and their parents. Tape-record them sometimes, or even video-record them if that facility is available.

Drawing

Children's first recordings will be pictures, and pictures should form part of their recording repertoire throughout their infant years. In all their schoolwork, give them practice in drawing what they see; their pictures of artefacts will then reveal a wealth of detail.

Writing

Try getting the children to put captions to your pictures, captions on their own pictures and captions on displays. Show them a variety of ways of committing information to a written record, and real examples of literature and information, written in the past, that we can read today. Include stories, letters, reports, poems and diaries. For example, to show the children the latter, discuss first what a diary is, and how diaries are the evidence of history as it happens. Tell the children that we still have copies of diaries written long before their grandparents were born and that these tell us about life long ago. (See, for example, *Being a child* Core Activity 2.) The diaries of John Evelyn, Samuel Pepys and Anne Frank are very famous, but are unsuitable for the very young. Try bits of *The Diary of Adrian Mole* and *Gilbert White's Year*.

Continually encourage the children to make records

of what they are learning, in the form of letters, reports, stories, diaries, poems and any other ways appropriate; and to not only write by hand, but to use machines like typewriters or word-processors. Keep this up, including the short captions, until the end of their infant years. It is not always necessary or important to write at length to deliver a message, and children (and teachers) need to appreciate this.

Acting
Acting has little do to with historical research, but letting children try to project themselves into time past in order to understand it better will enliven the learning process. For example, dressing in period costumes will help them to realise how restricting and uncomfortable some clothes must have been. Give the children plenty of opportunities to dress up, and also to do things in ways no longer practised.

CARRYING THROUGH THE RESEARCH PROCESS ▷

When some of the children in your class are experienced enough as researchers to carry through a very small project themselves, let them try. Here is an example:

Kings and Queens of long ago
Choose a King or Queen and ask the children to find out the following:
— What did he/she look like? What were his/her distinguishing features?
— What royal family was he/she born into? Who were Mum and Dad?

Afterwards, the children should say where they got the information and whether they consider the source reliable. They can then pose two more questions themselves and try to find the answers, commenting again on their sources. Their questions might be among these:
— Where did he/she live?
— What sort of a person was he/she?
— Who did he/she marry?
— Did he/she have children? What were their names?
— What is he/she remembered for? What is the evidence?

Let the children decide how they record their findings and how they present them to others.

FAMILY

TOPIC WEB

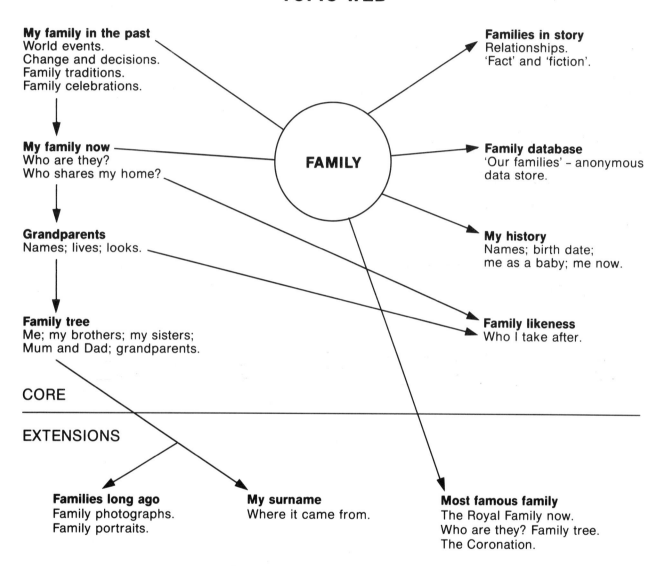

My family in the past
World events.
Change and decisions.
Family traditions.
Family celebrations.

My family now
Who are they?
Who shares my home?

Grandparents
Names; lives; looks.

Family tree
Me; my brothers; my sisters;
Mum and Dad; grandparents.

FAMILY

Families in story
Relationships.
'Fact' and 'fiction'.

Family database
'Our families' – anonymous
data store.

My history
Names; birth date;
me as a baby; me now.

Family likeness
Who I take after.

CORE

EXTENSIONS

Families long ago
Family photographs.
Family portraits.

My surname
Where it came from.

Most famous family
The Royal Family now.
Who are they? Family tree.
The Coronation.

THIS TOPIC AND THE NATIONAL CURRICULUM ▶

Work in this topic can be treated as part of a broader cross-curriculum theme with links including the following:

English All aspects
Mathematics Number; handling data
Science Genetics
Technology Design and construction of family belongings
Geography Community, population mobility

Creative arts
— *Art* draw, paint and model family likeness; look at and comment on family portrait paintings
— *Drama* feelings in families, impact of events on families

1

ABOUT THIS TOPIC

General points

● In all the topics in this book it is a good idea to use the children themselves, and their families, as your first point of reference. However, this is especially important with *Family* because history is about people and their pasts, and our family members are 'living resources' who can tell us about what has happened. Also, ordinary everyday things, like how people in the family got along together or who did the washing-up, are not widely documented. It may be possible to give children a sense of time, and family through time, using oral history alone, if you are offered sufficient information about particular families. Anonymous photographs and artefacts are your support materials if the families represented in your class cannot supply them. You can then add stories about families to help discussions of 'fact' and 'fiction'.

● Ask for parental support in answering questions and lending photos and memorabilia, and ensure the security of borrowed 'treasures' in your classroom.

● You may have to handle the issue of death in the family. There are books listed on page 3 which will help you to support and inform the children if they want to talk about this. You may judge these books as unsuitable for placing in the 'book box' for general access without discussion.

Family in recent history

The twentieth century is said to be one of rapid change. However, family life in Britain has not changed all that much. There are a few important trends to note. Wide availability of contraception, chances to take work outside the home (before the First World War one woman in three was a domestic servant), affluence, and the range of and access to kitchen appliances have changed the lives of women. However, women are still the pivotal figures in family life. They still do most work in the home, spend more time at home and make everyday decisions about home life. The very poor, whether men, women or children, are still, by comparison, as deprived as at the turn of the century. It may be that the memories of the families of children in your class bear out or refute these comments. They are a general overview, and not a pointer to trends in particular families or parts of the country.

RESOURCES

Family photos
Include some from the children themselves, and books and postcards showing family groups and mothers and babies from the beginning of the century to today.

Artefacts
Include, for example, some of the following:
— a family bible;
— heirlooms that are not fragile (perhaps a comb, a pipe, a pair of gloves);
— possessions that have special significance for a mum or grandad (ration books, school reports, tram tickets, Coronation mugs).

Reproductions of family portraits
Include, for example, some of the following:
Goya *Family of Charles IV*, 1800.
Ingre *The Stamaty Family* (pencil drawing), 1808.
Devis *The James Family*, 1751.
Zoffany *A Family Group in a Landscape*, c. 1775.
Gainsborough *The Baillie Family*, c. 1784.
Reynolds *The Fourth Duke of Marlborough and his Family*, c. 1776.

Story books
There are literally hundreds of books which would help to open up discussion about the children's families now and in the past. Those listed here are some starters.

Ahlberg, J. and A. *Peepo!*, Picture Puffin.
Baker, J. *Grandmother* and *Grandfather*, Andre Deutsch.
Blume, J. and Trivas, I. *The Pain and the Great One*, Heinemann.
Brandenburg, F. *Aunt Nina and her Nephews and Nieces*, Bodley Head/Piccolo.
Browne, A. *Piggybook*, Julia MacRae.
Cameron, A. *The Julian Stories*, Gollanz/Fontana.
Cherrington, C. and Northway, J. *Sunshine Island, Moonshine Baby*, Fontana Lions.
Chorao, K. *Oink and Pearl*, World's Work/Young Puffin.
Cole, B. *The Trouble with Gran*, Picture Lions.
Davis, A. *My Grandma the Monster*, The Women's Press.
Dupasquier, P. *Dear Daddy*, Andersen/Puffin.
Edwards, D. *All About My Naughty Little Sister*, Methuen.
Flournoy, V. *The Patchwork Quilt*, Picture Puffin.
Gould, D. *Grandpa's Slide Show*, Viking Kestrel.
Henkes, K. *Margaret and Taylor*, Viking Kestrel/Young Puffin.
Hoffman, M. and Burroughes, J. *My Grandma has Black Hair*, Methuen.
Hutchins, P. *Titch*, Puffin.

Hughes, S. *The Trouble with Jack*, Corgi.

McAfee, A. *The Visitors Who Came to Stay*, Hamish Hamilton.

Macdonald Denton, K. *Granny is a Darling*, Walker Books.

Macdonald, E. *John's Picture*, Aurum Press.

Perry, S. and Wildman, N. *Grannies and Grandads*, A & C Black.

Rogers, P. *From Me to You*, Orchard Books.

Smith, B. *Minnie and Ginger*, Pavilion Books.

Stevens, C. *Anna, Grandpa and the Big Storm*, Viking Kestrel/Young Puffin.

Swartz, A. *Her Majesty, Aunt Essie*, Picture Puffin.

Thompson, P. and Jacques, F. *Good Girl Granny*, Imago Publishing.

Van Leeuwen, J. *Tales of Oliver Pig*, Bodley Head/ Fontana Young Lion.

Waddell, M. *Grandma's Bill*, Simon and Schuster.

Waddell, M. *My Great Grandpa*, Walker Books.

Williams, M. *When I was Little*, Walker Books.

Books about death

Althea, *When Uncle Bob Died*, Dinosaur.

Burningham, J. *Grandpa*, Jonathan Cape.

De Paola, T. *Nana Upstairs and Nana Downstairs*, Methuen.

Varley, S. *Badger's Parting Gifts*, Andersen and Fontana.

Viorst, J. *The Tenth Good Thing about Barney*, Collins.

Information books

Coote, R. and Bentley, D. *My Parents* 'My Family' series, Firefly.

Crush, M. *The Family Tree Detective Book*, Young Library.

Morrison, I. A. *Her Majesty the Queen*, Ladybird Books.

Turner, D. *Queen Elizabeth II*, Wayland.

CORE ACTIVITIES

1 Starter discussion about family

Talk with the children about their families, and let them take turns in telling who is in their family and who shares their home. This will alert you to issues that will need sensitive treatment. For example, for those children who are with one parent or in care, you will need to plan work tasks to minimise embarrassment and exclusion.

2 Family names

Ask the children to find out the full names of their brothers and sisters, their parents' full names, and the names of their grandparents. If there is a good response to this, each child can draw up a simple family tree (see overleaf). If there are few responses or few 'traditional' nuclear families, use one or two sample families to show the children how to draw and find things out from a family tree.

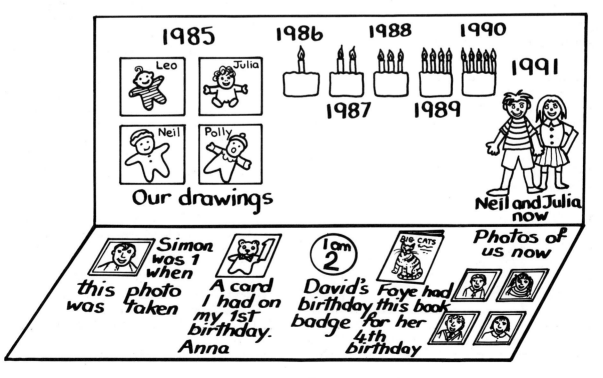

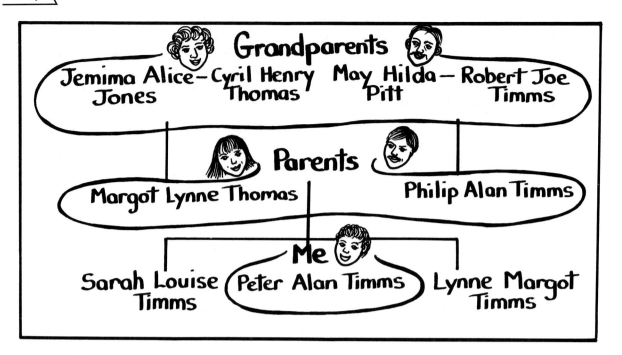

Copymaster 1 gives children the chance to draw a family tree.

3 Family stories

Read two or three stories about families with the children. Use these as sources of comparison between different families and relationships, and as starting points for the children to tell 'true' stories about their families. For example, in *Tales of Oliver Pig* there is a story entitled 'Grandmother's Visit' in which Oliver, his sister, Amanda, and mother prepare for her arrival. Having heard this, some children may be able to recount tales of visiting grandparents, and some grandparents may recall visitors they had come to their homes when they were younger. In *Peepo!* there is not only period detail in the pictures, but the rhyming storyline includes things the family members do, including grandma ironing. This should prompt discussion about who lives in the family home and who does various kinds of job at home. Again, children may be able to ask their grandparents how things were when they were younger.

4 Family traditions

Ask the children to find out, for example, what the family do when a new baby is born, when there is a birthday, when on holiday, on Christmas Eve, or for Sunday lunch (see below). Are there traditional first names, or expressions that are special to their family?

5 Family photos

Assemble a collection of family photos, from several decades, that the children can inspect and compare. Include pictures of their families (or your family) and postcards of Edwardian or Victorian families. Question them about how the people look, what they are wearing, their hairstyles, jewelry, footwear.

6 Ordering generations

Let the children put pictures of children, and adults, cut out of magazines or catalogues, in generation order. Make a class book or concertina book setting each generation in time.

Name	My family traditions
When?	What happens?

Changes in family life

My name_____	Name of person I talked to_____

Biggest changes (draw or write)

1.

2.

3.

7 'Happy families'

Make some large playing cards showing pictures of adults of different ages and children. Let the children invent activities to do with them. Here are some possibilities:

— Sort generations.
— Create a family tree using some of the cards and give everyone names.
— Shuffle the cards and pull out a few, create a family and write a story about them. (This allows a range of possibilities, including one-parent families and several generations.)

Copymasters 2 and 3 comprise pictures which can be made into playing cards, or illustrate family trees or displays.

8 Change in family life

Ask the children to find out from someone they know over the age of 60, the three biggest changes that have happened to their family life at home in their lifetime. Let the children list these on a simple record sheet (see above). The changes may be things like supermarkets, and family ownership of cars and television.

With the children's help group these replies and compile a composite display entitled 'In our grand-parents' lifetime'.

9 'Then and now' exhibition

Display items from the past that you and the children have collected, alongside things in current use. Invite the children to identify which things belong to previous decades, and discuss reasons for their decisions (see below).

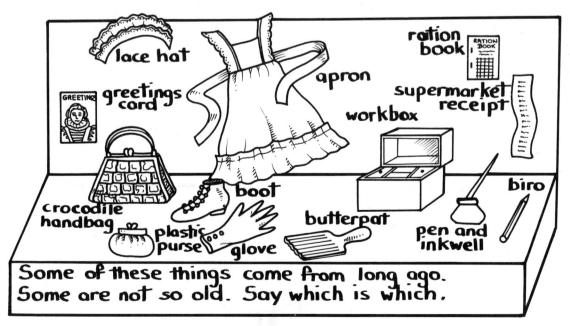

Some of these things come from long ago. Some are not so old. Say which is which.

Picture comparisons of artefacts are possible using **Copymaster 4.** In most cases the children will be able to 'place' the objects quite easily, but some should provoke discussion. For example, what sorts of food did the Victorians eat for dinner and how does it compare to what we eat today? Most houses today still have candles for emergencies and many have open fires.

10 Comparing generations
Ask the children to draw themselves, their mum or dad, and one of their grandparents, and to draw lines connecting obvious likeness between them. They could, for example, show likeness and differences in hair colour, eye colour, handedness, and height (see the illustrations above).

To go with their drawings, ask the children to write a little about what sort of person each one is and again to point out similarities and differences in personaility and mannerisms. You could structure their answers by letting them begin:

— 2 ways I am like my Mum (or Dad).
— 2 ways I am like my Gran (or Grandad).

Copymaster 5 invites children to record this comparison.

11 Family decisions
Have there been big decisions made in the family, the rationale for which the children can begin to understand? To find out you may need to send a short questionnaire home to parents. Do assure parents that the information is to help children understand that there are reasons for the ways people behaved in history, and that the decisions made in their own families have changed the course of their own family history. You will need to let parents know the kind of information you are looking for. For example, did part of the family emigrate after the war, has the family moved house, have there been changes of job, do the family now live distant from other relatives, and why have all these changes been made?

After the introductory explanation, you could set the question out like this: *What are the biggest changes that have happened in the (Smith) family since 1920? Please can you list up to five changes, and write why you think they occurred.* The replies will need collation, and you can discuss them with the children. If a family responds by giving a collection of events that are especially important to the local community, invite someone from the family to come and talk to the children, bringing memorabilia with them.

12 Family gatherings (parties and other events)
Find out from the children how their families celebrate. What is it like at a family party? What is expected of the aunties, the grandads and the children? Do the women always supply the food? Do the men always do the drinks? Are the oldest people in the family always waited on? Ask them to see if their grandparents can recall family parties and what happened at them. Let the children draw pictures to show what various people do and did. Sort and display their pictures. It may be that there is a tradition of separating roles of men and women at family parties, and longstanding traditions about what boys and girls wear and do.

13 Family database
Using appropriate software, create a simple family database. You will need to ask for parental permission to store information, and its anonymity needs to be assured, so you will have to assign each family a data-surname or a number. This will enable you to create and print family trees, and timelines showing family change.

14 Using dates and statistics
Find out some dates that are of importance to families this century. For example, frozen food arrived in 1924, television in 1925 and nylon in 1935. Talk to the children about the dates or statistics you have chosen and let them discuss their importance.

EXTENSION ACTIVITIES

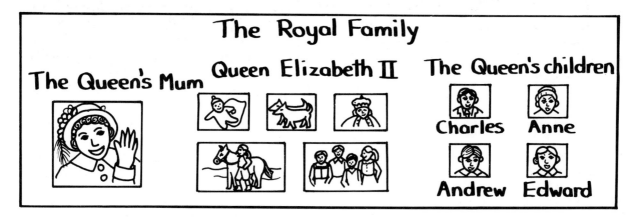

1 The Royal Family

Tell the children about our present monarch and her immediate family. Encourage the children to bring in pictures from the newspapers and magazines of various members of the royal family. Draw up a family tree of the House of Windsor (so named in 1917). Tell the children how the Queen came to succeed to the throne and who her likely successor is.

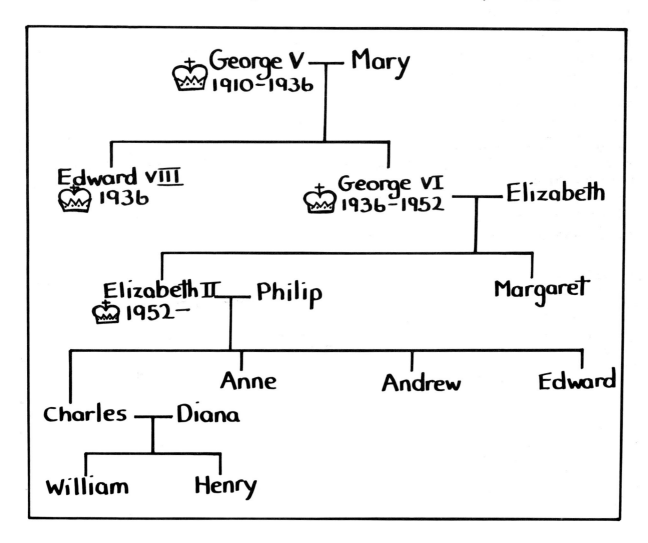

 # 1953 The Coronation and our families mug coin

The queen was crowned a long time ago, in 1953. The crown has jewels in it. Josh.

When the queen was crowned my family joined in a big party in the street. Louise

My Gran's got a mug with the queen on it. Yvonne.

The Coronation was in 1953, 10 years before my Mum was even born. Steve

Giles' family in Coronation Year

Reginald (my Grandad)
Audrey (my auntie)
Ted (my uncle)
Betty (my auntie)
Hilda (my Gran)

Giles says: My Mum was not even born when the Queen was crowned.

2 All about the Coronation
Children may have adults in their families who can remember the Coronation vividly. Find out what happened locally at the time of the Coronation. Let the children record what happened and set it in the context of their own families.

3 Family portraits (some famous paintings)
Make a collection of some reproductions of family portraits. Let the children inspect, interpret and comment on the families depicted.

4 Surnames
Help the children to trace the origins of their surnames. Discuss the tradition of a family line using the father's family name rather than the mother's.

Topic: Family. Suggested level(s) of work involved in activities

Core Activity Number	Level	Core Activity Number	Level	Extension Activity Number	Level
1	1	8	2	1	3
2	1/2	9	2	2	2/3
3	1	10	2	3	2/3
4	1/2	11	2	4	3
5	2/3	12	2		
6	1/2	13	3		
7	1/2	14	3		

HOMES

TOPIC WEB

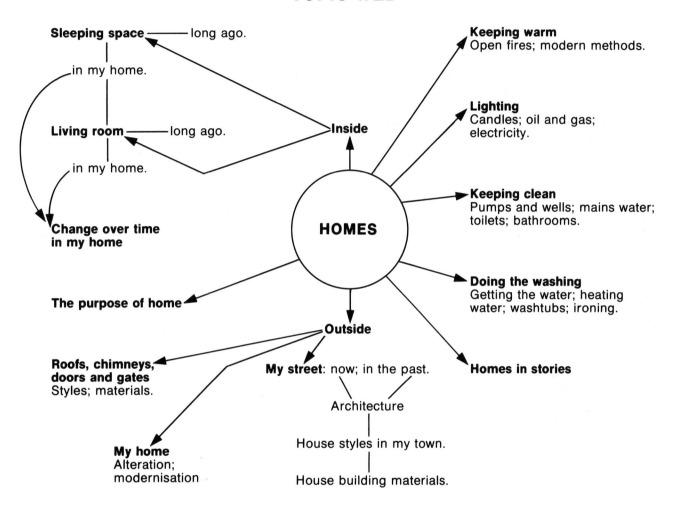

Sleeping space —— long ago.

in my home.

Living room —— long ago.

in my home.

Change over time in my home

The purpose of home

Roofs, chimneys, doors and gates
Styles; materials.

My home
Alteration; modernisation

Inside

HOMES

Outside

Keeping warm
Open fires; modern methods.

Lighting
Candles; oil and gas; electricity.

Keeping clean
Pumps and wells; mains water; toilets; bathrooms.

Doing the washing
Getting the water; heating water; washtubs; ironing.

Homes in stories

My street: now; in the past.

Architecture

House styles in my town.

House building materials.

CORE

EXTENSIONS

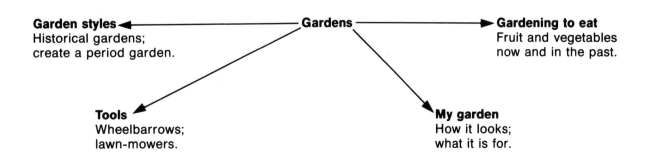

Garden styles
Historical gardens; create a period garden.

Gardens

Gardening to eat
Fruit and vegetables now and in the past.

Tools
Wheelbarrows; lawn-mowers.

My garden
How it looks; what it is for.

9

THIS TOPIC AND THE NATIONAL CURRICULUM ▶

Work in this topic can be treated as part of a broader cross-curriculum theme with links including the following:

English All aspects

Mathematics Handling data including measures; shape and space

Science Materials, animal homes

Technology House design and construction

Geography Community size and location, map making

Creative arts
— *Art* 'the built environment'; architectural styles; interior design
— *Drama* theatre based around the home (for example, an enactment of *The Three Little Pigs*); dance related to house building, strength and feelings about home (for example, security, protection, safety)

ABOUT THIS TOPIC ▶

General points

● Like *Family*, this is a topic which demands sensitive handling, particularly in a climate where people feel that their home life is open to criticism.

● There is much evidence that children's drawing follows a developmental path and that this is reflected in their drawings of houses. You may therefore find that some children will draw homes that more closely match their development than the actual home, or picture of one, that is placed before them. Despite this, children should be encouraged to observe and make comment, both orally and on paper, about homes they can see.

● You will need to explain to children that houses have changed in the way they look over many hundreds of years; and that sometimes you can tell how old a house is by looking at it (because it matches a 'style' that was the pattern for houses at a particular time), but sometimes you cannot (because the house is a copy of a style common a long while ago).

Homes in history

There are some important basic ideas about homes that apply throughout history. They are these:

— Home is a refuge, a place in which to feel secure and have some privacy, not only from outside but also personally; home is where we relax.
— Home life has a series of routines attached.
— Home has a value, that of the building itself, and of what it means to the people who live in it.

These are the threads through the centuries that the children should be helped to feel, for history is about continuity as well as change.

It seems likely that people first started building homes about 10 000 years ago. The first homes were like caves with a leaf or turf roof — materials which are close at hand have always been used in house building. About 7000 years ago home began to take on a long rather than round shape. This shape allowed the possibility of confining animals to one end while the family could live at the other, and also the option of creating partitions so as to add extra rooms to an original dwelling. Outside walls are likely to have been low in the first homes. The introduction and development of doors, hinges, handles, knockers, locks and gutters deserve discussion and research beyond the scope of this book.

Until about 1500 few homes had stairs. Early homes had a fire in the centre of the floor, with a hole in the roof for the smoke to escape. In Norman times fires were lit against outside walls, the smoke escaping through a flue cut in the wall. By 1500, chimneys are in evidence, and coal had begun to supercede wood as a fuel. It remained so until the introduction of oil and gas in the 1950s.

Light got into early homes through 'wind-holes' (hence window) and the open door. Glass was too expensive and therefore a luxury until the 1500s, and much later than that for the poorest and most rural communities. Oiled paper or cloth was placed at the windows to let in a little light and to keep out some of the draught. Candles, oil lamps improved by the discovery of paraffin in America in 1859, and gaslamps (from around 1840) served as artificial lighting. The invention and development of the electric light bulb by Edison and Swan (1878), transformed home lighting and, as electricity was made available, it was universally adopted.

It is through the homes of the wealthy that architectural styles developed and have been preserved. The homes of poorer people in Britain seem to have been subject to few changes over many hundreds of years, until this century. With the industrial revolution people moved into towns and homes were built for factory workers, but bathrooms and inside lavatories have only become part of any new house plan during the last 60 years. Until the 1950s homes had coal fires and no background heating. Since the war, oil-fired and gas central heating have become common. So too has a garage (and latterly a double garage) for the family car. The fitted kitchen is a product of the post-war years, and it is only in the last decade that some families have gone from acquiring a TV and refrigerator to installing a deep-freeze and dishwasher.

Gardens in history

Gardens as we know them occur in advanced civilisations where there is some wealth and leisure. The idea of a garden emerges with the start of agriculture, several thousand years B.C. As soon as communities began to be fortified, gardens appeared within the walls while agricultural land was left outside. The Domesday Book mentions gardens within city walls. Gardens were used at this time for growing vegetables, herbs and some fruit. Once it became less important for homes to be fortified, moated manor houses took the place of castles, and gradually even the moat became part of the garden and decorative rather than utilitarian. The 'typically English big-house' gardens, including box hedges, knot gardens and arbours, began to emerge.

Monasteries as enclosed self-supporting communities used the land to good effect, not only in producing all that was needed to eat but in setting out gardens of leisure. Herbs were very important in early gardens, for they not only added flavour (and vitamins and minerals) to food, but also provided medicines and had healing properties. Apothecaries' gardens became very elaborate, and their products were distilled to provide oils and mixed together in a pharmacy to make up doctors' supplies.

Plant containers have a long history for they were in use in some societies at least as early as 2000 B.C. We know the Romans used window-boxes. The earthenware flowerpot, like those we know today, was first made in the early nineteenth century, but it is now being replaced by plastic and paper-composition substitutes.

RESOURCES

Photographs

Include some of houses in the immediate locality of the school. If the school has a camera, take a roll or so of houses, showing a variety of age and style if possible. Without the children, walk around the streets near the school and note any unusual homes. If the community has a clearly identified centre, look for buildings of different styles here too. Look at local guides to trace any important homes that you have missed.

Pictures

Include interiors of homes in the past showing furnishings, lighting, heating, washing arrangements and how clothes were washed; and pictures of garden equipment, produce and styles.

Artefacts

Collect everyday objects found in homes in the past, for example, a flatiron, an oil lamp, a tin bath, a baize tablecloth, a reproduction of *The Light of the World*, a footstool, old newspapers, and old kitchen utensils.

Story books

There are plenty of traditional stories, rhymes and songs which include homes, published in a variety of editions; for example *The Three Little Pigs*, *Hansel and Gretel* and *The House that Jack built*. Classic stories may yield descriptions of homes; for example, Miss Havisham's house in Dickens' *Great Expectations* and the house in *Tom's Midnight Garden* by P. Pearce. Try songs too, like 'When father papered the parlour!' and 'This Old House'. Listed below are a few more book titles.

Andersen, H. C. *The Old House*, Abelard Schumann.
Brighton, C. *The Picture*, Faber.
Macdonald, E. *The Two Sisters*, World's Work Ltd.
Muller, G. *A Garden in the City*, Macdonald.
Reyes, G. *et al.*, *Once there was a House*, Collins.
Rockwell, A. *In Our House*, Heinemann.
Rogers, E. and P. *Our House*, Walker Books.

Information books

Johnson, J. *Our Garden Year*, Orchard Books.
Launchbury, J. and Montford, S. *History on your Doorstep*, Young Library.
Lines, C. *Exploring Houses and Homes*, Wayland.
Pace, C. and Birch, J. *Homes*, 'Look Around You' series, Wayland.
Ross, S. *Where we Lived*, 'Starting History' series, Wayland.

CORE ACTIVITIES

1 Homes in stories

Make a collection of stories in which the home is pivotal, ranging from baby Jesus' first home in the cattle stall to the homes of the witch in *Hansel and Gretel*, the giant in *Jack and the Beanstalk* and the pigs in *The Three Little Pigs*. Additions to these traditional tales could come from your own stocks and the suggested list in the *Resources* section. Let the children experiment with paint, crayon, collage and other media to produce a range of pictures of homes. Discuss and sort these homes into, for example, those suitable for big families, the cold and draughty ones, the most comfortable ones. Display these in a 'gallery' alongside the children's comments (overleaf).

Homes in Stories

This home does not look comfortable. Cindy

I bet this was cold in winter. Ali

Is the roof made of straw? Sonia.

I think this is a home for a princess. Molly

My Gran lives in a house like this. The rooms are small. Mark

The Three Pigs

The House that Jack Built

The Giant's Castle

Baby Jesus

Hansel and Gretel

Stories we love

2 What is home?

In stories, home is not always an hospitable place, and this may be the case for some children in real life too. Be sensitive to this possiblity and discuss with the children what home means to them, why they have a 'Home' in chase games, and the idea that people have always needed homes. If the children are ready for some 'time jumping', ask them to begin to think about what sort of homes we would have if, for example, there were no modern tools, if rocks were the only material we had, if wood was readily available. Start a display about what a home is.

3 My home on the outside

Ask the children to draw what their house is like on the outside. They can draw in class or at home; or you could get permission to walk the class to the home of one of the children so that they can all draw that. From their drawings they can arrive at an 'essentials' list for homes. Add this list to the 'Home is' display (below).

4 My street

Using the register, locate where most of the children live. Choose two or three streets and let the children make drawings of some of the buildings there.

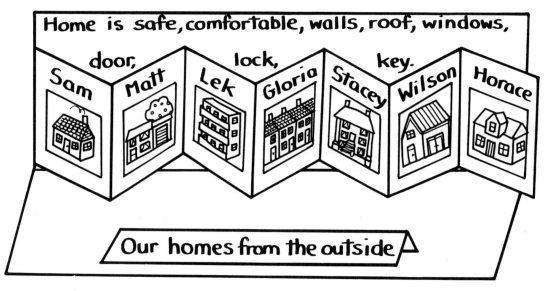

Home is safe, comfortable, walls, roof, windows, door, lock, key.

Sam   Matt   Lek   Gloria   Stacey   Wilson   Horace

Our homes from the outside

5 My street long ago

If it is appropriate, and they are available, show the children pictures of what their community looked like some years ago. Display these pictures alongside the children's comments (written up by you) and some pictures of what the street looks like now.

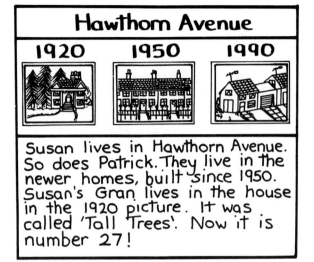

Hawthorn Avenue

1920   1950   1990

Susan lives in Hawthorn Avenue. So does Patrick. They live in the newer homes, built since 1950. Susan's Gran lives in the house in the 1920 picture. It was called 'Tall Trees'. Now it is number 27!

6 Unusual houses in my area

Quiz the children about which they feel are unusual houses near the school. If possible let them take you to look at those they mention. Construct a timeline with buildings of the periods represented in the neighbourhood and discuss this with the children. Let them put some photos of local houses in time order.

7 Building materials

Let the children say what their own house is built from, what other building materials are in use in local homes, and chart the materials used alongside comments about whether they are or were locally available.

Copymaster 6 is a timeline worksheet related to house building styles (an ancient highland stone-walled cottage with a turf roof; an Elizabethan timbered house; a modern house with a double garage; a Saxon dwelling; high-rise blocks of the 1960s; a Georgian house; a Victorian terrace).

8 Roofs and chimneys, doors and gates

If this is appropriate, on the basis of your preparation research, let the children observe and compare roof materials and chimney styles, door and gate designs and put these on a timeline. **Copymaster 7** provides pictures of doors which can be stuck onto drawings of appropriate homes.

9 'Living space' in my house

Ask the children to describe their living space to their friends. Let them fill in a simple record sheet to say whether their home is open-plan, has separate rooms, and the kinds of things the family do in each of the rooms. **Copymaster 8** can be used as a record sheet for this activity. Talk with the children about those things found in their living rooms which would not have been found in homes in the past.

10 Homes at the beginning of the century

Show the children some pictures of Victorian and Edwardian interiors, and ask them to compare them with what they have said about their own homes. Mount a display which highlights the comparisons.

1910   1991

Look for the differences
— amount of furniture
— colours and styles

11 'Sleeping space' in my house'

How many bedrooms do the children's homes have? Is there a bathroom and airing cupboard upstairs? What are their beds like? Let the children describe and draw some aspects of the upstairs in their house. Compile a book about 'Our homes upstairs' using the children's drawing and pictures from magazines.

upstairs in my house there are 3 bedrooms and a bathroom
Leslie
Toys
Lego
Leslie

Our 'Upstairs' Book

12 Upstairs long ago

Look with the children at pictures of the interiors of homes from long ago. Discuss the differences between these and their own homes. Include the points that, long ago, people did not have an 'upstairs', that they may have shared their home with animals, and that there were vast differences between the sleeping space for poor and rich people. Put the pictures you look at in time order, and make it clear that many of them came well before the lifetime of the oldest people alive today.

13

Keeping warm

Fire with no hearth

Gas fire

Fire on a hearth

Homes long ago

Josie's house is warmed by electricity.

Sarah's home has gas central heating.

Terry has an open coal fire at home.

13 Heating homes

Talk with the children about how they keep warm at home. If there is a range of methods in use, these could be charted in a block-graph. Discuss the development of home heating, from open fires to the use of gas, oil and electricity. Look at pictures of Victorian and Edwardian interiors where fires can be seen. Examine and compare some old advertisements for, for example, gas fires with those currently in the gas showrooms. Help the children to use folded card to produce living-room pictures showing the heating (above).

14 Lighting homes

Tell the children about the dangers of electricity, both in appliances and in flexes and plugs. Show them an electric light-bulb and a plug and explain how they work. Tell the children about gas lighting and, if possible, show them some old photographs in which the gas mantles can be seen. There may be an elderly person in the community or a great-grandparent who remembers gas lighting, and can be asked about it and recorded on tape. An old oil lamp, and a candle in a holder can be shown to the children to complete the lighting cycle. All these objects can be put on a timeline.

15 Keeping clean now and in the past

If you have a sink in the classroom it may be possible to mount a display around that! (See below.)

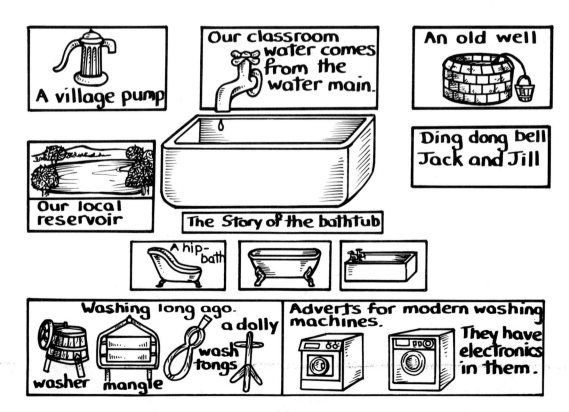

A village pump

Our classroom water comes from the water main.

An old well

Our local reservoir

The Story of the bathtub

Ding dong bell Jack and Jill

A hip-bath

Washing long ago.
a dolly
wash tongs
washer   mangle

Adverts for modern washing machines.
They have electronics in them.

14

In any case, begin with a visit to a sink and a discussion of how the water gets there, whether it is hot or cold, where the water supply comes from and what we need water for. Discuss where water is supplied in the children's homes. Remind them of all the possibilities, including garden and garage taps, the washing machine and dishwasher, the kitchen and bathroom sinks, the bath and shower, and the toilet. Compare this service with times before there were water mains when people used street taps, pumps, streams, springs and wells. Discuss the possible ways of heating water without a modern boiler. Let the children speculate on the probable extent of bathing and washing when supplies of water were difficult to get.

Keeping the house clean may form part of the discussion, and the invention of the vacuum cleaner in 1901 represents the most important addition to the range of cleaning tools.

16 Doing the washing

Link this activity with the previous one and talk about the problems of doing the washing by hand. Show the children pictures of women doing washing in the past. An old mangle or washboard would be a useful resource for the children can, under supervision, try these out. Show the children pictures of irons used before electric irons were available.

Copymaster 9 is an activity sheet about doing the washing. In a Victorian kitchen or laundry the children would have found the mangle, washtub, dolly, bar of soap and washboard. Clothes were soaped and rubbed on a washboard, which was usually a board made of hardwood with a fluted surface that helped to remove the dirt. A dolly was a wooden appliance with two arms, and legs or feet, used to stir clothes in the washtub as the water was heated. Before the washing was hung up to dry, much of the excess water was wrung out of it with a mangle.

17 A review of houses long ago

If you have done many of the sixteen given activities, opportunities will have occurred to talk about homes in previous centuries. It may be helpful to the children to review what they have gleaned about life long ago and to order their information in epochs. For example, a simple picture quiz about ways of keeping warm, a missing-word puzzle about how homes were set out, or pictures of homes with clues in them about what the homes are built from and how they are lit and heated,

will alert you to gaps which you may feel should be filled in the infant years.

Copymaster 10 is a stimulus for story writing about how an everyday object finds its way into a museum.

18 Changes made to my house

This activity may prove inappropriate for children in your present class. However, those children whose families have lived in their house for a long time could take home a brief questionnaire about house alteration/ modernisation. Some families may know from the deeds when the bathroom was put in or the garage built on. Below is a suggested layout for the questions. Discuss the results with the children and, if the information about a particular house is full enough, create a picture story of the house showing the sequence of changes and additions, with suggested reasons for them.

19 Using dates and statistics

Choose some dates and statistics of interest to the children and use them as the basis for discussion. Here are some examples:

Dates of introductions or inventions	
Bricks (from Holland)	1400s
Chimneys and stairs (in poorer homes)	1500s
Sash windows	1600s
House numbers (made compulsory in London)	1765
Letterboxes in front doors	1840
Yale locks (invented by Linus Yale)	1848
Principle of the electric light-bulb (invented by Thomas Edison)	1879

% of families having	*1970*	*1981*
fridge	66	93
telephone	37	75
central heating	30	59
freezer	4	49

How my house has changed

Address _____

When built _____

Changes inside	Dates
Changes outside	

EXTENSION ACTIVITIES

1 My garden

If a fair proportion of the class have gardens, ask them to find out some things about them. For example: 'How big is your garden – does it 'fit' the width of the house, or go beyond that? Do you get puffed running to the bottom of your garden? What grows there? Are there plants and trees that have been there many years? What goes on in the garden – is it for the dog to run in, for you to play in, for growing food?' Those children who have no garden could team up with children who have, and make a record of the garden. A sample record sheet is set out on **Copymaster 11.**

2 Gardening to eat

Investigate the kinds of edible things grown in gardens. Make a collection of fruits, vegetables and herbs (or pictures of these and dried herbs) available to people in, for example, medieval England, Georgian times and now. Look for garden/allotment plans from these periods of time and compare them.

3 Garden style

If there is a stately home in the locality, with a garden that is preserved, look at the layout of the garden and find out which patterns of planting were popular when the garden was created. Also, try to discover how many people were garden servants employed in maintaining the garden in its heyday.

4 Creating a garden from history

With the help of a local gardening group or a parent who is an enthusiast, help the children to create a garden which replicates one from the past. A herb garden would be a good example. Try drying the herbs grown and using them in old recipes. This is an extended project which needs constant maintenance and sustained interest.

5 Garden tools: wheelbarrows and lawn-mowers

Ask the children to design and build a miniature wheelbarrow from Lego®, balsa wood or junk materials. Let them make comments on each other's designs, and the kind of job they would be appropriate for. Search for designs and styles of wheelbarrow (first referred to around 1340), both in history and in current production, and find out about their construction and usage. The children could also build replicas and compare them with their own designs.

Find out about the invention and development of the lawn-mower, from Edwin Budding's model of 1830 to those in current production.

Topic: Homes. Suggested level(s) of work involved in activities

Core Activity Number	Level	Core Activity Number	Level	Extension Activity Number	Level
1	1	11	1	1	2
2	1	12	1/2	2	3
3	1/2	13	1/2	3	3
4	2	14	2/3	4	3
5	2	15	2/3		
6	3	16	2/3		
7	3	17	3		
8	3	18	3		
9	1/2	19	3		
10	2/3				

COMMUNICATION

TOPIC WEB

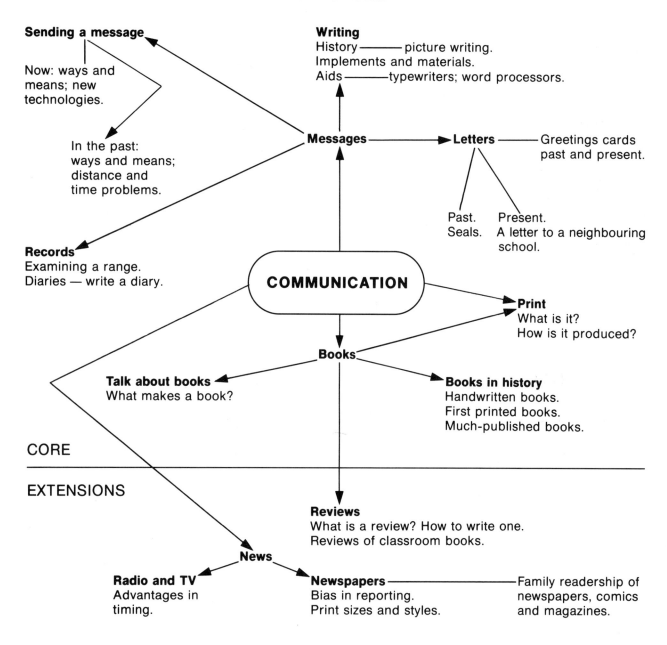

Sending a message

Now: ways and means; new technologies.

In the past: ways and means; distance and time problems.

Records
Examining a range.
Diaries — write a diary.

Writing
History ———— picture writing.
Implements and materials.
Aids ————typewriters; word processors.

Messages ⟶ **Letters** ——— Greetings cards past and present.

Past.   Present.
Seals.   A letter to a neighbouring school.

COMMUNICATION

Print
What is it?
How is it produced?

Books

Talk about books
What makes a book?

Books in history
Handwritten books.
First printed books.
Much-published books.

CORE

EXTENSIONS

Reviews
What is a review? How to write one.
Reviews of classroom books.

News

Radio and TV
Advantages in timing.

Newspapers ————————— Family readership of newspapers, comics and magazines.
Bias in reporting.
Print sizes and styles.

THIS TOPIC AND THE NATIONAL CURRICULUM ▶

Work in this topic can be treated as part of a broader cross-curriculum theme with links including the following:

English   All aspects
Mathematics   Abstractions, codes and ciphers
Science   Information technology
Technology   Communication systems
Geography   'Location', addresses, maps

Creative arts
— *Art*   Lettering, design and layout
— *Drama*   Message-taking; the story of a letter
— *Music*   Conveying 'messages' through music (how, for example, rhythm, tempo, pitch and tone change the 'meaning')

ABOUT THIS TOPIC ▶

General points

● The challenge in this topic is making the history of communication relevant to young children. Three of the really important milestones are the discovery of writing, which really is too long ago for it to have any meaning to infants; the invention of printing; and the current technological revolution which we are in the middle of and which will, eventually, transmit the *spoken* word in the form of print.

● The two main areas for focus in this topic are messages (both spoken and written) and their delivery; and keeping a written or printed record in newspapers and books.

● The children will know that you value reading and writing. Be sensitive to those children who may already feel they are failing in these areas, and to the fact that some children come from homes where there are adult illiterates.

Messages and signals

Smoke signals, semaphore, and flags all predate the work of Morse in sending messages by electric telegraph (1838). Radio, invented in 1895, and television, first demonstrated in 1926, use electromagnetic waves which travel at the speed of light. Thus news can be relayed as it happens. The first international TV broadcast was the Coronation in 1953. Video recording was first achieved in 1956.

The history of writing and print

Out of communication through drawings arose the earliest writing, scratched into wet clay 5500 years ago.

There was a gradual shift in different cultures from pictures to symbols, to syllables, and finally to single letters or sounds. Our alphabet is based on that of the Romans, with the addition of J, U and W in the Middle Ages.

Quill pens were in common use from about 800 to the 1850s, when wooden pens with a metal nib became popular. Fountain pens have been available since the turn of the century. Ballpoint pens and felt-tips are more recent inventions.

For thousands of years messages and books had to be handwritten. Producing books was lengthy and arduous; few people had access to them so few learned to read. Though there is evidence of wooden blocks in use for printing in 868 in China, it was not until the 1400s that metal blocks were used in Germany. William Caxton set up his press in England in 1475. Nowadays, type is transferred from computer to paper by laser and then photographed onto a printing plate.

The first European newspaper was printed in Germany in 1609. *The Times* was established in 1785. Steam-driven printing presses, put into use by *The Times* in 1814, made rapid printing of newspapers a reality.

The postal service

Systems of letter carrying were set up by kings for their own use, and letters sent by other means were seen as possible treason. Though England has had a postal service since 1635, the work of Rowland Hill and the introduction of the 'Penny Black' adhesive stamp in 1840 marked the start of a universal penny post. Postcodes arrived in 1959.

RESOURCES ▶

Artefacts
If possible, include:

— an old typewriter and a word processor;
— old greetings cards and postcards belonging to the children themselves and from as early a date as possible. (There may be a collector among the children's parents, or a local group of enthusiasts who would make loans from a collection.)

Books
Provide books published long ago (at least before 1920) and some hardback children's and adult books recently published, with which to compare them.

Information
There are many sources of information, including:

— the Post Office for the postal services currently available;

— pictures from and of the past, for example stage-coaches can be found on Christmas cards;
— copies of local and national newspapers, including some from long ago and recent issues;
— written records, including, for example, the register, the school log-book, school reports (either your own or some old ones made anonymous), written receipts and diaries.

Tools and materials
Obtain as many of these as you can:

— writing implements like sticks, quill pens, dip-in pens and water-based inks, brushes, pencils, crayons, chalks, fountain pens, biros and felt-tips;
— surfaces to write on, including slate, clay, fabric, and paper of various weights;
— print-making materials, including suitable 'blocks', paints and paper;

— examples of print of various sizes and styles, including illuminated lettering.

Story books

Most stories of relevance to this topic are about postal services. Here are a few starter titles:

Ahlberg, J. and A. *The Jolly Postman*, Heinemann.
Grace, J. *Portland Bill's Important Message*, Purnell.
Graves, R. *The Big Green Book*, Young Puffin.
Hedderwick, M. *Katie Morag delivers the Mail*, Bodley Head/Picture Lions.
Cunliffe, J. The *Postman Pat* books, Andre Deutsch/Scholastic.

Information books

Aliki *How a Book is Made*, Bodley Head/Hippo Scholastic.
Browne, A. *I Like Books*, Walker Books.
Cobb, V. *Writing it Down*, Hodder and Stoughton.
Dixon, A. *Paper*, from the series 'Threads', A & C Black.
Macdonald 'Starter' *How Writing Began*.
Matthews, R. *Communicating by Signs*. See also other books in the series 'Signs and symbols', Wayland.
Merrison, T. *Books*, 'Media story' series, Wayland.
Thomson, R. *A Book*, 'Making' series, Franklin Watts.

The Post – a leaflet from The Royal Mail about their 150th anniversary (1990).

CORE ACTIVITIES

C12 –16

1 Oral culture

Discuss with the children what life would be like if no-one could read or write. Let the children speculate about what people did before many people were literate. Look at some of the disadvantages of oral culture alone. The important points here are that communication between communities is intermittent, and all that people know can only be told orally to their children and grandchildren. Point out that there are still some oral cultures in the world, in remote parts of third-world countries, and that even in so-called developed countries (including Britain) by no means every grown-up can read and write.

2 Oral messages now

Discuss with the children the ways in which we can deliver a message. These include:

— Telling face to face with words or signs.
— Telling at a distance using:
   a sign medium (for example smoke signals, drum signals)
   a messenger   intercom
   a telephone   personal radio.

Let the children act out 'face to face' messages, and look at the use of signs for the deaf and the signals made by using, for example, semaphore, flashing lights in lighthouses, road signs. Discuss with them the disadvantages, including lack of distance and confidentiality and, in the case of some signals, the lack of detail in the message. Create a display of some of the ways of sending messages (see below).

Talk about how technology has revolutionised the sending of word messages at a distance and the possible users of various methods. The biggest users are people in business. For example, some of the children may have parents who have a mobile phone or use electronic paging (carry a 'bleeper' which calls them to a phone). You may be able to invite a parent in to show the children some office machines and how they are used, and to demonstrate electronic paging.

3 Sending oral messages long ago

Delivering an oral message long ago carried many disadvantages, including the limits on distance and time and lack of confidentiality, even if the messenger went on horseback. Let the children enact the delivery of such a message which brings news that *was* secret, but was entrusted to a perfidious messenger or arrives too late (perhaps news of a king dying, or a great battle).

Get the message?

Signs for the deaf   Flags – semaphore   Some roadsigns   A lighthouse sends a flashing signal   More road signs   No parking at any time

19

Egyptian hieroglyphics	Lesley's message	Chinese writing	Mamuna's code	Our alphabet
(hieroglyph symbols)	(eye → eyes; sun, stick figure)	木 川 子 月 白 馬 水 子 日 林 川	⦀ ⫽ ⎮ — ⫽ ⎮ — — ⦀	A B C D E F G H I J K L M N O P Q R S T U V W X Y Z

Ask Lesley and Mamuna about their made-up writing

4 How writing began

How do the children think the first writing came about? Let them experiment with pictures and symbols to create their own messages. From this activity should come a discussion about writing being a 'code' which has to be understood by all those reading it, hence the development of alphabets and standard spelling. Display the children's codes along-side, for example, Egyptian hieroglyphics (with an interpretation), Chinese letters (with their meanings) and our own alphabet (see above).

Copymaster 12 can be used to record children's picture writing.

5 Writing: tools and materials

Focus on writing implements and materials, and let the children try writing with sticks, canes, home-made brushes, feathers, dip-in pens, pencils, ballpoints and felt-tip pens. Display the results of their efforts (see below). Look at which implements were available many centuries ago, and which have only been in use since Victorian times.

Let the children try writing in clay, on slates and stones and various qualities of paper. Talk about where messages are, even now, put onto materials which were in use in the ancient world, for example, a vase or decorated flowerpot where marks have been made in the clay, headstones on graves, house numbers carved in slate.

6 Paper-making

Discuss the process required in paper-making. Make some recycled paper in school – there are well laid out instructions in *Paper* by A. Dixon (see *Resources*).

7 Aids to writing

Look at the development of the typewriter and word processor, and the importance of these in business. Let the children have a go at typing and/or word processing their own letters and stories. Make a class book of these.

Telex, teletext, fax and viewdata are all relatively recent developments in the transmission of typed information. Some of the children may know about these through the work their parents do. Help the children to find out more about these facilities. Though they may seem beyond the experience of small children, they are a part of the world into which they have come and they represent that sector of our knowledge in which change is most rapid.

We write and draw with these

Which is the oldest?
Which did Victorians use?
Which do you use most?

quill pen
crayons

Eliza wrote her name with:
pencil Eliza
dip-pen Eliza
chalk Eliza

chalks
pencils
dip-in pens
charcoal   biro
felt-tips

Take one and try writing.

Please put the display things back

Eliza says, 'Pencil is easiest. Dip-pen is very difficult.'

20

8 Sending letters in the past

Explore past ways of sending written messages, including by foot-messenger, on horseback, and using a postal service. Discuss the use of a seal in ensuring that the message remained unopened (we still say an envelope is sealed). Let the children create their own seals, either with sealing wax or commercial modelling material. Tell the children about the establishment of the penny post. Begin a display about 'Sending written messages'. **Copymaster 13** is a record sheet for seal-making.

9 Sending messages now

Find out about the current postal service and other contemporary ways of sending written messages, including door-to-door deliveries and the ways in which typed messages can now be sent through telex, fax and modem. Add this information to the display 'Sending written messages'.

Copymaster 14 lets the children create a timeline of message delivery.

10 Letter writing

Written messages become important as soon as they have personal relevance. Show the children the conventions of letter writing, and liaise with another school so that they can exchange letters. Make a class book of letters and replies.

11 Sending greetings

Show the children pictures of, or real, Victorian greeting cards and holiday postcards. Discuss the kinds of pictures, the rhymes, the postage paid, and compare them with a selection of contemporary cards. Add all this information to your display.

12 Keeping records

Writing is important as an aid to memory. Handwritten records that you can show the children include diaries, the school log, church records and birth certificates. Assemble a collection of current and past records for the children to look as and talk about.

Copymaster 15 allows the children to create a diary for one particular day of the week (say Tuesdays) over a period of time.

13 What is print

The principle of print is to put ink or paint onto a block which is then pressed onto paper, fabric or another surface. Let the children experiment with making their own printing blocks, using ends of boxes, potato-cuts, string, etc. If they press these into foam sponge made damp with paint, prints can be produced with them. The points they should grasp are that once a block is made it can be printed up any number of times, and that the block is always the reverse of what is printed. Discuss the implications of these ideas for the printing of fabric and, until recently, books and newspapers.

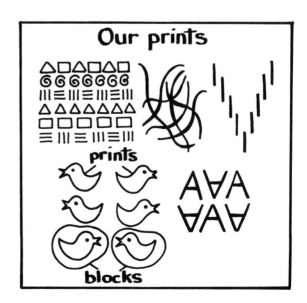

14 What makes a book

Look with the children at a selection of books. Tell the story of how a book is conceived and who is involved in producing it. Explain the technical terms like cover, spine, author and title, and the ISBN numbers and dates in the front. Discuss the kinds of books there are. Look at some old books, including some from before 1900. Discuss the range of books available to us now, compared with those available in Victorian times.

15 Books in history

Tell the children about handwritten books produced before there was print, including illuminated manuscripts, and about some of the books which, though written long ago, are still 'best sellers' (including, for example, the Bible, Shakespeare, Gilbert White). See if you can get hold of several editions of some of these, to show the children that a printed book can not only be produced in vast numbers and various editions over years, but that they also provide a way of communicating with people many hundreds of years in the future.

A book with illuminated letters in it.

Copymaster 16 invites the children to add their initial to decorated panels and to try illuminating initials of their choice.

◄ EXTENSION ACTIVITIES ►

1 Family news across the world now

The telephone revolutionised the sending of family news. The children can investigate how calls can be made to all parts of the world using international codes. Let them look some of these up, but do warn them of the bills involved if they try them out!

2 National and international news

Radio and television are now so advanced that national and international news can be shown while it is being made. We can see the Olympic Games, World Cup Football, disasters, rescues, even wars, as they happen. Ask parents if their children may watch a children's news programme on television for a couple of days. Let the children comment on 'live' and 'pre-recorded' reports.

3 Newspapers

Investigate the history of newspapers, comics and magazines. Ask the children to find out which newspapers, comics and magazines are read in their house. What did their grandparents read when they were younger? Get hold of a very old edition of a local newspaper and compare its coverage with a current copy.

4 Print style and size

Investigate the variety of sizes and styles of print used in books and magazines, and compare these with those used in some old copies of *The Times* and old books (you may be able to find a book with 's' printed as 'f'). Discuss the clarity and size of text in use now with that used long ago. Display samples of print and books for the children to look at (see below).

5 News bias

Choose an item of interest from the local news during the recent past. Collect press cuttings giving accounts and opinions. Talk to a few local people who have opinions on it (the dinner ladies may be able to comment). Help the children to sort out the facts and the opinions. Discuss all the different people's points of view and how they were represented in the news.

6 Reviews

Show the children what a book review is. Select a number of books for review and let the children independently review some of them. Collate the reviews and duplicate them so that all the children may read them. Discuss the fact that the reviews reflect a variety of opinion, and that information books and newspapers similarly reflect the views and interpretations of different writers.

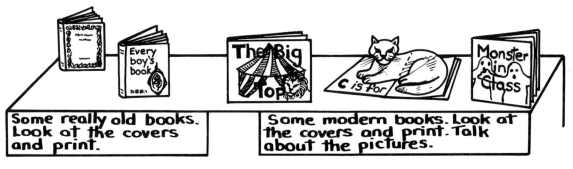

Some really old books. Look at the covers and print.

Some modern books. Look at the covers and print. Talk about the pictures.

Topic: Communication. Suggested level(s) of work involved in activities

Core Activity Number	Level	Core Activity Number	Level	Extension Activity Number	Level
1	1/2	9	2	1	2
2	1/2	10	3	2	3
3	2	11	2/3	3	3
4	2	12	3	4	3
5	1/2	13	1/2	5	3
6	2/3	14	2	6	3
7	2/3	15	3		
8	1/2				

CLOTHES

TOPIC WEB

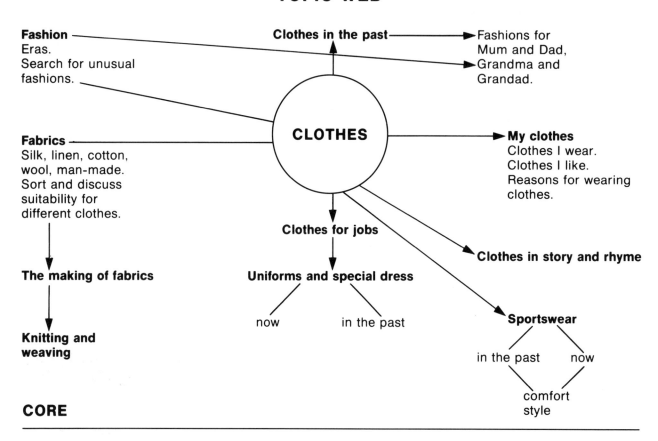

Fashion
Eras.
Search for unusual fashions.

Clothes in the past → Fashions for Mum and Dad, Grandma and Grandad.

CLOTHES

→ **My clothes**
Clothes I wear.
Clothes I like.
Reasons for wearing clothes.

Fabrics
Silk, linen, cotton, wool, man-made.
Sort and discuss suitability for different clothes.

Clothes for jobs

Clothes in story and rhyme

The making of fabrics

Uniforms and special dress

now   in the past

Sportswear

in the past   now

comfort
style

Knitting and weaving

CORE

EXTENSIONS

Hats
Research and make hats from the past.

Create a class collection.

Dyes

Natural   Man-made

try and compare

Shoes
Collect, examine and discuss.

Materials used.
Range of styles.

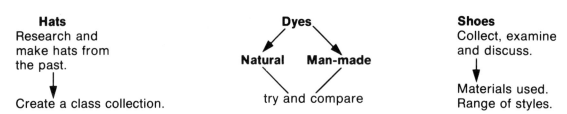

THIS TOPIC AND THE NATIONAL CURRICULUM

Work in this topic can be treated as part of a broader cross-curriculum theme with links including the following:

English   All aspects
Mathematics   Measures, sizing/cutting patterns
Science   Natural and man-made materials
Technology   Yarn to finished garment; spinning, weaving, knitting and sewing
Geography   Cotton, flax and silk-growing locations, sheep farming; locations of industries producing man-made fibres

Creative arts
— *Art/design*   drawing and designing clothes and costumes; costume in paintings
— *Drama*   story and rhyme where costume is pivotal; the art of disguise
Health Education   Clothes and shoes to allow comfort and growth

ABOUT THIS TOPIC ▶

General points

● Be sensitive to the children's own state of dress, for as you begin to focus on what they are wearing they may become more aware of those who are scruffy or in designer clothes. The fashion industry seems to reach some quite young children, causing peer-group pressure and the risk of ostracism.

Clothes in history

Clothes have and still do commonly serve several purposes, namely:

— they protect our bodies from harm and extremes of temperature;
— they satisfy the prevailing ideas about modesty and attractiveness;
— they demonstrate vanity, power and affluence, or lack of it;
— they identify membership of a tribe, nation, caste, profession or other group.

In addition, clothes have sometimes been specifically adapted to take account of the activities people do when wearing them. 'Fashion' has only recently become accessible to people other than the rich.

The step from using skins and leaves as covering to wearing cloth came about when spinning and weaving were invented. It is not known how or when this began, but we do know that the Chinese were spinning silk in about 3000 B.C. and that linen was used by Egyptians at about that time.

Before the Industrial Revolution, spinning was done at home, commonly by women. Men were more often the weavers. Natural dyes have been common knowledge for many centuries. Some places in Britain became known for a dye originally produced there, hence Lincoln Green. Key dates include 1764 (the spinning-jenny) and 1854 (the Singer sewing machine).

RESOURCES ▶

Artefacts

Obtain as many of these as possible:

— a spindle, spinning wheel and loom for the children to look at;
— items of clothing worn in the past, supplied by the children's families, your family, or from jumble sales, private collections or the Museum Loan Service;
— a shoemaker's last, and a collection of footwear.

Pictures and photographs

Include postcards or other reproductions of period paintings showing figures in period dress; and pictures of people now and in history, in a variety of costumes, from magazines, catalogues, newspapers and books. Add photographs of people this century, including those that the children bring in of members of their own families, and pictures from old editions of local and national newspapers of people in ceremonial and everyday dress. Some newspapers regularly carry historical pictures. Look also for pictures of sportswear, hats and footwear from long ago and the present day. Finally, add some pictures depicting the ways in which fabrics are produced.

Materials and tools

Provide equipment necessary for dyeing fabric, and some garments to dye (see *Extension Activities*). A collection of raw material and fabric pieces, including leather, raw wool and raw cotton; linen, silk, wool, nylon, and polyester thread and fabric; and fabrics suitable for hat making.

Story books

Bradman, T. *The Sandal*, Puffin.
Neitzel, S. *The Jacket I Wear in the Snow*, Julia MacRae.
Rodda, E. *Something Special*, Angus and Robertson.
Zeifert, H. *A New Coat for Anna*, Julia MacRae.

Information books

BBC TV-watch, *Clothes*, BBC Heritage Books.
Cooke, J. *Costumes and Clothes*, Wayland.
Crawford, S. *How Clothes are Made*, Wayland.
Jobin, C. *All about Wool*, Moonlight Publishing.
Marshall, P. *Clothes*, Macdonald.
Sichel, M. *History of Men's Costume*, Batsford.
Ross, S. *What we Were*, 'Starting History' series, Wayland.
Woodbridge, R. N. *Cotton* from the series 'Threads', A & C Black.

1 My clothes

Talk with the children about the clothes they are wearing, why they wear clothes at all, and the reasons for the choice of fabric. Let the children draw what they are wearing, along with some of the other things that are the favourites in their wardrobe. Each child can create a folder or concertina book.

Copymaster 17 allows the children to picture-record why they wear clothes; that is for warmth/coolness, for protection and to indicate 'membership' (see *About this topic*).

2 Clothes in stories

Collect together a range of illustrated books in which clothes are pivotal to the story, for example *Little Red Riding Hood*, *The Emperor's New Clothes*, *Puss in Boots* and *Oh, Soldier, Soldier*... Discuss the importance of the clothes in each story.

3 Fabrics past and present

Assemble a collection of fabrics. Let the children do a variety of 'sorts' using the fabric pieces, and record their 'sorts'. Use these as the basis for a discussion about the fabrics' origins, whether they are man-made or natural, the kinds of clothes they would be suitable for, and whether they would have been available in the past. If you have an expendable collection of fabrics, you could let the children create a timeline of fabrics, attached to models or pictures of people (see below).

Copymaster 18 gives the children themselves the chance to record the results of their 'sorts'.

4 'Fabric' from animal skin

Tell the children about how animal skins are treated so that they can be used to make leather shoes, bags and coats. Discuss how people in ancient times probably dressed, and why they wore clothes. Talk about the declining use of animal furs to make coats.

5 Making fabric from wool

Tell the children that sheep's wool has been used to make clothing since prehistoric times. See if the children can name any other animals whose coats provide fibre for making clothes. They may name, for example, goats, rabbits, llamas. Show the children some raw sheep-wool and some spun wool that is in a ball. Explain the process of spinning (necessary because wool fibres are short) using a spindle and spinning-wheel. Explain that nowadays this process is mechanised. If you have a supply of wool and a spindle, let the children have a go. If not, find out if there is a local group with an interest in crafts, for example the Women's Institute, where there may be someone who will demonstrate spinning by hand to the children. Once the wool is in a ball it can be knitted or woven to make a fabric.

6 Knitting and weaving

If there are particularly skilful children in your class, you may consider asking a 'mum' who knits conventionally and well to show the children how it is done. They may like to look at some finished garments together and identify the stitches used. Some children may like to try doing garter stitch.

Let the children try weaving on home-made looms.

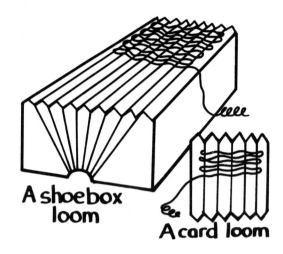

7 Where cotton and silk come from

Following Activity 3, the children may already know where cotton and silk originate and what they look like. Mount a small display showing, for example, a picture of silkworms, silk thread and silk fabric; and a cotton boll, a reel of cotton thread and a cotton dress. Explain that cotton and silk have been used to make clothes in some parts of the world for several thousand years.

8 Man-made fabrics

Show the children some samples of man-made fabrics and talk about their history and the ways in which they are produced.

9 Clothes for jobs now

Choose several jobs for which people wear special or distinctive clothing or a uniform. Assemble pictures of these and let the children look at them carefully. Guide their comments to include discussion of fabric, colour, practicality and purpose. Display the pictures and the results of the discussion.

10 Clothes for jobs long ago

Building on Activity 9, assemble a collection of pictures of people wearing distinctive work-clothes in the past. Let the children observe and discuss these, and compare them with work-clothes of today. Mount a display to accompany the one from Activity 9.

11 Timeline: work clothes

Collect a variety of pictures of people in work-clothes, both contemporary (from catalogues and magazines) and from the past (book illustrations, postcards, reproductions of paintings). Invite the children to make a timeline using these pictures, and discuss their efforts. Display the outcomes of the children's work. **Copymaster 19** provides pictures which could be added to this timeline or used to form an additional task for children to do individually. The pictures show medieval peasants; Tudor servants; eighteenth-century servants; Victorian servants; a prewar housewife and a factory worker from the same time; and modern office and factory workers.

12 Grandma's and Grandad's clothes

With the children, look at photographs and other illustrations of men and women in clothes of all the decades from the 1920s to the 1960s. Choose some aspect of dress, for example length of skirt or style of jacket, and trace what happened to its appearance over those decades. Discuss the idea of fashion. Make sure that the children know that fashion has, until very recently, been the prerogative of the rich, and that fashion sometimes reflects people's attitudes and what is happening in history. If the children can supply photographs of members of their own families in 'period' clothes, display these alongside pictures of those same people nowadays.

13 Mum and Dad in fashion

Ask the children to bring in photographs of their mums and dads, especially in their teens. The resulting discussion will depend on whether they are wedding pictures, holiday snaps, or 'everyday' pictures. Look closely at the fabric, styles and 'image' of the clothes. For example, do they look comfortable? Are they like the clothes Mum and Dad wear now? Do Mum and Dad have different clothes for different occasions?

14 Sportswear then and now

Look at pictures of sport and games in the past. You may have access to pictures of ancient civilisations, or to pictures of tennis players and football players before the war. Compare the styles adopted with their modern equivalents, which can be found in newspapers, magazines and sports catalogues. The children should be able to comment on which styles would make the games easier to play and which are more modest. Mount a display, including some of the children's and/or their parents' own sports gear (opposite).

15 Strange fashions

Fashions tend to emphasise or draw attention to particular parts of the body. Some fashions, including those in living memory, have been extremely uncomfortable. You and the children could do a 'search' for the most uncomfortable fashions in history. The children may find out, for example, about the periods in which ruffs, hoops, corsets, platform shoes, winkle-pickers and mini-skirts were the rage. If appropriate, link this to Activity 12.

16 'Then and now' exhibition

Assemble a collection of clothes from several generations ago to the present day. The children's families may be able to supply things. A mini-skirt and 'flower power' beaded dress are just as good as a flapper fringe-dress and feather boa. Display the items so that the children can handle them, comment on them, and compare them with current fashions. Remember, the clothes do not need to come from long ago to offer the children a sense of the past and change over time.

17 Dressing up

Borrow some period costumes for children from a local dramatic society. Let the children handle them, try them on, draw each other wearing them, and comment on them in terms of comfort, ease of movement, warmth, modesty, attractiveness and impact. If only adult clothes are available, try them on yourself and your colleagues. The children will never forget how they looked!

EXTENSION ACTIVITIES ▶

1 Dyes: natural and man-made

Let the children investigate some of the natural dyes that have been available for many centuries. These include, for example, onion skins, some mosses and lichens, fruits and berries. Find out what was used to 'fix' the dyes. With adult help, let the children try dyeing fabric using ancient dyes. Cotton sheeting, men's handkerchiefs or tee-shirts would probably take the dye well. Look also at some of the constituents of man-made dyes, and try using these. Display the results (see overleaf). The dyed fabric can then be used to make, for example, puppets, purses, shoe-bags, etc. as well as forming the backdrop to a collage.

Fabrics dyed with natural dyes.

We tried natural and man-made dyes.

Fabrics dyed with man-made dyes.

We used these fruits and vegetables.

We used these man-made dyes.

onions blackberries grapes

dye

2 Hats in history

With detailed resourcing, children can look at the headgear worn by men and women through several centuries. Using felt, card, wire, tissue paper and other materials, they can then create some 'period' hats. A sumptuous classroom collection, for subsequent use in drama, might include the following:

— a tricorn hat;
— a 'Gainsborough' hat with a large floppy brim;
— a lace-trimmed bonnet;
— a 'Napoleon' hat.

Invite a milliner to come and show the children how hats are made. Trace the customs of raising your hat and wearing a hat in church.

3 Shoes in history

Assemble a collection of shoes. Make a foot-measure like those found in shoe shops. Discuss shoe sizing and research the size of people's feet in previous centuries. Discuss style and comfort in footwear, and the effects of ill-fitting shoes. Do a 'search' for footwear styles in history. List the kinds of materials used in making footwear, including wood (clogs) and rubber (wellingtons), and how the latter got their name.

Topic: Clothes. Suggested level(s) of work involved in activities

Core Activity Number	Level	Core Activity Number	Level	Extension Activity Number	Level
1	1	10	2/3	1	3
2	1	11	3	2	2/3
3	1/2	12	2/3	3	3
4	2	13	2/3		
5	2	14	2/3		
6	2/3	15	2/3		
7	2	16	2/3		
8	2	17	2/3		
9	2				

TOYS AND GAMES

TOPIC WEB

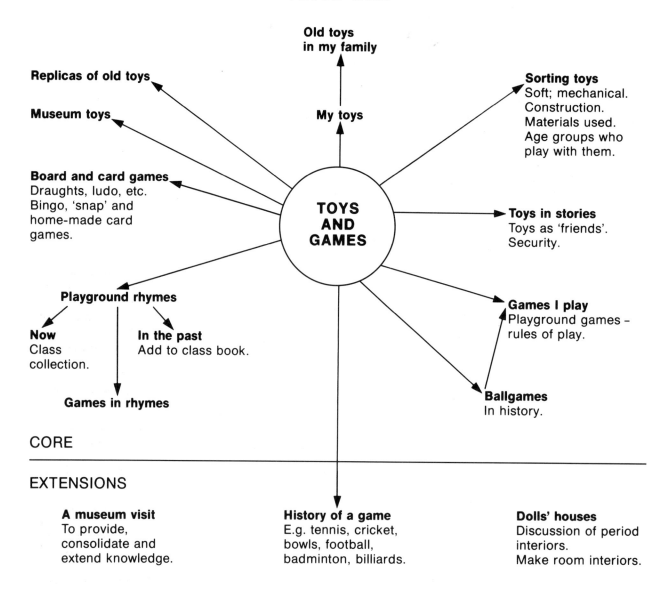

Old toys in my family

My toys

Replicas of old toys

Museum toys

Sorting toys
Soft; mechanical.
Construction.
Materials used.
Age groups who
play with them.

Board and card games
Draughts, ludo, etc.
Bingo, 'snap' and
home-made card
games.

TOYS AND GAMES

Toys in stories
Toys as 'friends'.
Security.

Playground rhymes

Now
Class
collection.

In the past
Add to class book.

Games in rhymes

Games I play
Playground games –
rules of play.

Ballgames
In history.

CORE

EXTENSIONS

A museum visit
To provide,
consolidate and
extend knowledge.

History of a game
E.g. tennis, cricket,
bowls, football,
badminton, billiards.

Dolls' houses
Discussion of period
interiors.
Make room interiors.

THIS TOPIC AND THE NATIONAL CURRICULUM ▶

Work in this topic can be treated as part of a broader cross-curriculum theme with links including the following:

English   All aspects
Mathematics   Number in counting games and scoring;
   Shape and space using construction toys and game
   playing
Science   What makes toys 'go'?
Technology   Model-making, for example, puppets
   and room interiors
Geography   Countries of origin of toys and games

Creative arts
— *Art/design*   drawing and making toys, board and
   card games
— *Drama*   playground drama, games and rhymes,
   re-enacting stories, for example, *The Tin Soldier*,
   Tottie, *Superted*
— *Music*   nursery rhymes and playground chants

ABOUT THIS TOPIC

General points

● Toy care – remind the children that toys are precious to their owners and so they must take care in handling them.

● Talk to the children about 'aging'. Toys from forty years ago may look uninviting but they were good to look at at the time.

Toys and games in history

Many of the toys available today and games played nowadays were known thousands of years ago. The table below shows some familiar toys and games and something of their history.

Toy or game	Dates	Information	Toy or game	Dates	Information
Dolls	2000 B.C.	Ancient Egypt	Boats	c. 2000 B.C.	Clay
	600 B.C.	Greece	Soldiers	1000	Arrived with the Normans
	1100	Pierotti family make doll in Italy		1893	Hollow-cast lead soldiers
	Middle Ages	Carved wooden dolls made in Germany and Holland	Puppets	c. 1300	Manuscripts show children watching puppet shows like the Punch and Judy, still seen today
	1825	First dolls with eyes that close			
	1836	Walking dolls made in Paris		1662	Pepys recorded seeing Punch and Judy
	1970	Action Man®		c. 1790s	Stick-puppets, Harlequin and Columbine, Jack-in-a-box
Doll's crockery		Evidence near Hadrian's Wall			
				1850s	Pollock's toy paper theatres
Dolls' houses	c. 1700	As playthings in Britain, though models as 'art' were made earlier, and a model house has been found in Europe dating from Neolithic times (3000 to 1800 B.C.)	Alphabet bricks	Elizabeth I	Children taught to read using these
			Noah's Ark	c. 1600	Thought to originate in Germany
Teddy bear	1903	Named after American president, Teddy Roosevelt, who saved a bear cub while on a hunting trip. Large-scale manufacture began in Germany	Jigsaw	1760s	A teacher at Harrow school cut up a map of the British Isles and asked the children to remake it
				1900s	Fretsaw used in jigsaw production
Panda	1936	First panda arrives in a Western zoo, toy replicas made soon afterwards	Rocking-horse		Hobby-horses date from thousands of years ago; rocking-horses are not so old. Charles I had one
Animals on wheels	1100 B.C.	Iran			
			Trains	1920s	Soon after the building of railways came models (see Peter's model in E. Nesbit's The Railway Children)
Kites	200 B.C.	China			
Construction toys	1901	Meccano®			
	1950	Lego®			
Balls, rattles	Ancient cave-dwellers	Made from dried fruit/animal bladders	Clockwork toys		In mass production in Victorian times, using tin

31

Game	Dates and information	Game	Dates and information
Five-stones	These were known to the Romans.	*Cup and ball*	*c.* 1500 France
Hockey	Known to be played in England in 1277.	*Cards*	1440 Printed with four suits and court cards, in France.
Tennis	Known to Shakespeare (see *Henry V*).	*Ludo*	1898
		Monopoly®	1935

RESOURCES

Artefacts
Provide a selection of toys that the children bring in, together with those borrowed from the school toy box. The selection should include the following:

a doll	a pull-along toy
a teddy	a dolls' house
soft toys	a wind-up toy
model soldiers	a battery-operated toy
farm animals	an electronic toy
Lego®	marbles and five-stones
building bricks	bat and ball
a jigsaw	a hoop
card games	a top

Add toys that belonged to parents and grandparents, or descriptions of them and dolls'-house furniture.

Books and catalogues
Obtain favourite books, including old ones and some reproductions of old ones; and toy catalogues, both old and new.

Pictures and postcards
Provide some depicting children with toys, or playing games, including a reproduction of the painting by Pieter Breughel entitled *Children's Games* (this can often be found as a print for wrapping paper).

Story books
Many stories and other books about toys include anthropomorphism to the extent that toys have adventures and face dilemmas, just as children do. For this topic the appropriate books give hints about the functions of toys in children's lives. The list below includes a few to start the children thinking.

Edwards, D. Some of the stories in *Mark the Drummer Boy*, for example 'Roger's Trains' and 'The Secret Teddy Bear', Methuen/Magnet.
Fisk, N. *The Model Village*, Walker Books.
Galbraith, K. O. *Laura Charlotte*, Hutchinson.
Hoffman, M. *Ip Dip Sky Blue: Playground Stories*, Collins.
Hughes, S. *Dogger*, Picture Lions.
Jacques, F. *Tilly's House*, Picture Lions.
Jonas, A. *The Quilt*, Julia MacRae.
Wildsmith, B. *ABC*, Oxford University Press.

Books containing rhymes and chants are much easier to find. Here are a few suggestions that may prove useful.

Ernest, E. (Ed.) *The Kate Greenaway Treasury*, Collins.
Greenaway, K. *Under the Window: Pictures and Rhymes for Children*, Octopus Books.
Lobel, A. (Compiler) *Gregory Griggs and other Nursery Rhymes*, Hamish Hamilton.
Opie, I. and P. *The Lore and Language of Schoolchildren* and *Children's Games in Street and Playground*, Oxford University Press.
Provensen, A. and M. (Illustrators) *The Mother Goose Book*, Beaver Books.
Stones, R. and Mann, A. *Mother Goose comes to Cable Street*, Picture Puffins.

Information books

Deshpande, C. *Five Stones and Knuckle Bones*, A & C Black.
Schofield, A. *Toys in History*, Wayland.

CORE ACTIVITIES

1 My toys

Ask the children to each bring in a toy for a 'Toy Day'. If you make it just one day, you will not have problems with those children who want to play all the time, or who remove other children's toys from a display, or who insist on taking their toy home each night. For that one day let the children take turns to talk about their own and others' toys, view them all and draw some of them. There may also be time to let the children rank some of the toys in order of preference and invent names for toys (like 'Scoop' the sand-digger and 'Eargone' the rabbit).

Mount a display to show the results of 'Toy Day' (see bottom of page). The display itself can yield further work for the children to do.

2 Sorting toys

Using the assembled toy-box toys, and some of the children's toys if they will allow, let the children do a variety of sorts and discuss the basis for their decisions. For example, they could sort and comment on the following:

— the age-range for which the toys are most appropriate;
— toys for boys and toys for girls;
— what the toys are made from.

These sorts have important implications for a study of toys in history.

3 Toys handed down to me

There may be children in the class who have toys that once belonged to someone in their family who is now grown up. Ask if it is possible for them to bring in those toys and tell their story. Make a class book about them.

4 Parents' and grandparents' toys

Ask the children to find out from their parents and grandparents the toys that they remember having when young. If there is little information from the children, take in toys belonging to you and your colleagues and let the children describe and discuss them.

5 Toys in stories

Select a variety of stories about toys, past and present. Read them to the children, or let them read them for themselves, and talk about the stories. Can the children relate them to their own experience? Do the stories show how toys are treated and what toys are for? Do they tell us about times past? Examples of appropriate stories include *Dogger* by Shirley Hughes and *Laura Charlotte* by K. O. Galbraith. (See the story books listed under *Resources*.)

6 Museum and picture-book toys

Do a search to find pictures of toys in the past, in picture books. Secure the help of the Schools' Library Service and the Museum Loan Service in getting information. You may even be able to borrow some old toys for the children to look at. Make a timeline of the pictures (see top of page 33).

Copymaster 20 children are required to ring toys that are out of period in a picture of Victorian children playing. The incongruities are the electric robot, remote-control car, Monopoly, felt-tip pens, model electric train, Action Man®, My Little Pony and the calculator.

7 A toy list

From their own experience, and if they have done some of the Activities 1–5, the children will now know something about a whole range of toys currently available and played with in the recent past. Help the children to begin a display collating all they know about the various kinds of toy. Tell them a little about which toys have been available for thousands of years,

and which are relatively 'new'. Create a partitioned display, with all that the children discover about the toys in appropriate sections (see bottom of page).

8 Making replicas of old toys

Invite the children to consult the display they started for Activity 7 and try ways of making replicas of ancient toys. For example, they could wrap cloth around little sticks or pegs to make dolls; make clay dolls and horses out of Newclay®; make balls with raw wool and soft fabric; and make rattles using shells, sticks, seeds and raffia. They could also make a hobby-horse by filling an old sock with newspaper and then tying it onto a stick. Eyes, ears, mane and mouth can be glued on, and bridle and reins can be tied to the head to complete the toy.

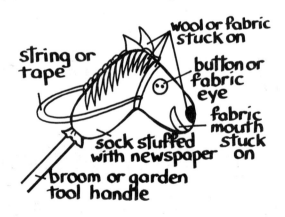

Let the children try making a paper theatre, like that produced by Pollock, using a shoebox and card. **Copymaster 21** shows how to make a card-and-paper theatre. **Copymaster 22** gives picture instructions for making a pantin (paper puppet). To make the pantin's arms move at the pull of a string, you need to attach the arms to a piece of thread and then attach a second piece of thread to the centre of the first, so that it hangs down the pantin's back and on below the feet. Pull the second thread for movement.

9 Create a toy museum

Use the toys the children have made in Activity 8 to create a 'Museum'. Point out that it is a museum of *replicas*, and that historians need authentic evidence before they can say such toys were actually around long ago. Then historians and archaeologists, using the little bits of things they find, sometimes make replicas so that we can see what the things really looked like. Create a display 'cabinet' to place in the entrance hall or where other children in the school can see it.

10 Playground rhymes we know

Ask the children to record on tape some of the playground rhymes they know. Let them write these down and illustrate them, and collate them into a book for the book corner and as a school resource.

11 Rhymes of the past

Let the children choose, enact and write out traditional rhymes to create a class book to set alongside 'Rhymes we know'. These could be spoken onto tape by the children, so that they can listen and read the text; or they could be made into a frieze for the classroom or corridor wall. Remember not to hang them too high above the children's eye-level. **Copymaster 23** provides the children with a decorated page on which to record rhymes they know and/or rhymes of the past.

12 Games in rhymes

Do a search of old rhymes to find a mention of games, for example: *Come with a hoop, come with a ball'*. Let the children compile a class or group book of old games, with pictures showing how they were played. **Copymaster 24** is a record sheet for an old game.

13 Games I play

Let each child choose three or so games that they enjoy playing outside, and ask them to draw or paint pictures or cartoons of themselves playing these. Mount a display showing the pictures and the rules of the games. Ask some of the children to demonstrate how their games are played during a PE session. There is much impetus here for drama work about games, rules, winning and losing, all of which could provide material for an assembly.

14 Ballgames in history

Using some of the games mentioned in Activity 13 as a starting point, help the children to discover the origins of the games and whether the rules have changed over years.

15 Breughel's games

Mount a large reproduction of the painting *Children's Games* by Breughel. Hang it low down on a wall where children can get close up to it. Let them use magnifiers to spot all the games being played.

16 Board and card games in history

Draughts and ludo are example board games to investigate and play. Have the rules always been the same? Is there an expert player among the children? Begin, as always, with games the children know. Do not overlook games from around the world if there are children in your class who know and can play them.

The set of cards with four suits and court cards dates back to about 1400. The children may like to assemble a number of sets and spot the differences, and they can also research and compare some early card designs. Then they can design their own and, using the photocopier and coloured pencils, create a class card pack. Encourage them to find out the names of games that have been played in the past with cards like this, and to play some games they know like 'Beggar my neighbour' and memory games.

17 Inventing a new game

The children can attempt to invent a new game which must include some of the elements of a game in the past.

18 Toy catalogues

If you can get hold of an old toy catalogue, let the children compare this with toys in catalogues available nowadays.

EXTENSION ACTIVITIES

1 Game search

Let the children choose a game in which they are interested. Here are some suggestions: tennis, cricket, bowls, football, badminton, billiards. They should research the date their chosen game was first played, the original rules, what the players wore, and other important facts. They can then write about the current state of the game. Their work could be presented on stand-up folders cut in the shapes of a bats and balls.

2 Dolls' houses

Assemble a collection of dolls'-house furniture, a borrowed dolls' house and craft materials, along with pictures and photographs of interiors from the past. Talk about the ways dolls' houses are furnished and how carefully the furnishings match what we call a 'period' in history. Invite the children to choose the time when their Gran was little, or when Victoria was queen, or another period after 1700. Then let them choose a room in a house and list ten things they would find there. Help them to find out what these things would have looked like and to make models. These can be placed in a shoebox room of the period. The models do not need to be intricate, but capitalise on the fact that making even a simple model of, say, a heavy Victorian saucepan, a hip-bath or flatiron will require observation, and discussion of an historical kind. In this discussion there will be opportunities to learn about the cooking 'range', the difficulties in bathing and how ironing was done. Display the interiors alongside pictures and photographs. The children may also realise that dolls' houses were expensive toys, really only available to wealthy families.

3 Museum visit

This could be an extension or core activity which begins or ends the topic. Take the children to see toys in a museum. Here are some suggested collections to visit:

The Bethnal Green Museum of Childhood, London.
Pollock's Toy Museum, London.
The Museum of Childhood, Edinburgh.
The Museum of Childhood, Menai Bridge, Anglesey.
Sudbury Hall Museum, Derbyshire.
Playthings Past Museum, Rednal, near Birmingham.

Other museums often have some toys so it is worth finding out about general collections.

Topic: Toys and games. Suggested level(s) of work involved in activities

Core Activity Number	Level	Core Activity Number	Level	Extension Activity Number	Level
1	1	10	2/3	1	3
2	1	11	2/3	2	3
3	1/2	12	2/3	3	1/2/3
4	1/2	13	2/3		
5	2	14	3		
6	2/3	15	2/3		
7	2	16	2/3		
8	3	17	3		
9	3	18	3		

THIS TOPIC AND THE NATIONAL CURRICULUM ▷

Work in this topic can be treated as part of a broader cross-curriculum theme with links including the following:

English   All aspects

Technology   Design, construction and style in school buildings, 'child friendly' design

Geography   Schooling across the world

Creative arts
— *Art*   drawings and paintings of the school and its environment

Philosophical and moral issues; for example, what schooling is for, what should be learned at school, alternatives to school

ABOUT THIS TOPIC ▷

General points

● In some ways this is the most sensitive topic of all because one of the chief functions of infant schooling has to do with the social and moral education of children. Clearly we want children to place a high value on schooling and we do not want them to be exposed to ideas which undermine the teachers, teaching or schools of today. By asking children to describe and discuss their current daily experience, and compare this with other times, we are putting schooling itself at the centre of moral debate. This is really a point to which you should be alert, so that you can be aware of your own values and thus be unbiased in discussion with children.

● There is a view common in current public debate that standards in education are lower now than in the past. This rather depends on what your standards are (see *Schools in history*, following). However, many of the parents of the children you teach may still hold that schooling is 'not as good' as when they were at school, and you need to be aware of the effects of these views on the children themselves. The interpretation of change and the notion of progress in education are ideas which demand your time before you start this topic with the children. (Discussion of the National Curriculum and the 'standards' debate can be found in *The Really Practical Guide to National Curriculum 5–11*, David and Wendy Clemson.)

● Girls have fared less well than boys in the history of schooling and it can be argued that, comparatively, that is still the case. Though it is in secondary schooling that this is most evident, it is through our attitudes to children and their work and worth in their primary years that the important values are taken on by children. Teachers are all-important in persuading boys and girls that education is vital, liberating and enlightening. Do not sell the girls short!

School in history

Children have, from ancient times, been taught to make their own way in the world. Their teachers have been parents or 'foster' parents, for in medieval times it was common for children of aristocratic parents to live their childhood in another family. Thus most children learned in the home (boys to earn a living, girls to keep house). Religious education was important too, and 'song' schools were established in which priests taught boys reading, writing, and singing for church purposes.

During the 15th and 16th centuries, much education still had a religious base. However, it was also increasingly seen as having social import, as a key to social mobility; it helped to create 'gentlemen and women'. Scholarship was seen as part of the educational curriculum. Discipline was severe and children were beaten into learning. In Tudor times aristocratic boys were still sent away from home, but to school and university rather than to learn the arts of war, as in medieval times. Elementary education was carried out by a variety of people who also worked at other jobs; and some schools were 'free' while others were fee-paying. Parish schools were viewed as a way of preparing the children of the poor for employment and it was from these schools that the idea of charity schooling emerged.

In the late 18th century a system called 'monitorial schooling' was introduced. Senior pupils oversaw the work of the younger ones, hence the word 'monitor', which is still used in some schools today. In fact, the reason why the teacher's desk was sometimes on a dais was so that the teacher could keep an eye, not on the children, but on the monitorial teachers.

Poor Law reform and provisions within the Factory Acts of the early nineteenth century made education a possibility for all the children in England. Education was, however, neither compulsory nor free, and until 1870 it was in the care of purely voluntary groups. Standards were established in Robert Lowe's *Revised Code* of 1862. Standard V in reading was achieved by reading aloud from a reading book in use with children in the first class in the school. This clearly is not comparable with the standards young children are required to meet under the National Curriculum.

It was not until this century that all teachers were expected to have undergone extra study, training or education in order to teach. For example, in 1880 the majority of 'teachers' were pupil teachers. Education reform early this century culminated in the Education Act of 1944, firmly establishing a continuous three-stage education system, along with the '11-plus' examination. The Plowden Report of 1967 revealed a wide range of provision and circumstances in primary schools and teacher-training establishments. The mid-twentieth century saw the adoption of ideas about definite sequential stages in children's development and the view that learning should be active and take account of the child's predilections. The National Curriculum makes for curriculum-based rather than child-led learning, and may lead to a reversion to a preoccupation with test results and achievement, rather than the realisation of potential.

RESOURCES

Artefacts
The following will give you a good 'base':
— old school books and equipment to set alongside modern equivalents;
— a camera and film to record a 'picture' of children in school now;
— old school prizes and reports.

Photographs and postcards
To set alongside the artefacts, obtain old photographs of teachers, children, classrooms and schools; school photographs belonging to members of the children's families; and postcard reproductions of paintings of children at school. Examples of the latter include the following:

Geoffrey *L'heure de la rentrée*
Rankley *The Dame's School at Christmas*
Vautier *Children Leaving School*

Story books
Many books about school that appeal to young children seem to be slightly 'wacky' and removed from 'real life'. Amongst the caricatures and unlikely events, the routines common in schooldays can be looked for and talked about. The few titles below are a starter list.

Ahlberg, J. and A. *Starting School*, Viking Kestrel.
Ahlberg, A. *Mr Tick the Teacher*, Viking Kestrel.
Barry, M. S. *Simon and the Witch*, Fontana Lions.
Blacker, T. *The Ms Wizz Books*, Pan Young Piper.
Carpenter, H. The *Mr Majeika* Books, Young Puffin.
Heaslip, P. *Starting School*, Methuen.
Lingard, G. *Frankie's First Day*, Andre Deutsch.

Information books
Clarke, A. *Finding out about Victorian Schools*, Batsford.
Stoppleman, M. *Schoolday*, 'Turn of the Century' series, A & C Black.

CORE ACTIVITIES

1 My class
With the children's help create a pictorial record of the class. There is a wealth of data here which you can collect in a number of ways. Here are some examples:

— As a whole class, do some head-counts (for example, six-year olds).
— Assign each of a number of groups a particular fact-finding exercise which contributes to a whole class collation. If each group is armed with a class list, they can find out from everybody one category of information. Examples might include:

Are you related to anyone in this school? If so, who is it and what is the relationship?
Do you live near school?
Did any of the grown-ups in your family come to this school? If so, who?
How do you get to school?

You will need to show the children how to do tallying, and transfer and interpretation of information. Discuss with them the general conclusions of their research. The findings may indicate things like the following:

— Most children have only brothers and sisters in the school (which has implications for lack of concentration of family members in a small area, and for family size).

— Most children live within two streets of the school (which has implications for the age and composition of the community, and the size of community that the school serves).
— Many children's parents did not come to this school (which has implications for mobility).
— Many children come to school by car (which has implications for family affluence, mums working outside home, and the range of choices available to families).

All the findings can be compiled into a class book, which will become an historical document in its own right in time. If you have at your disposal the school logbook and record and register entries, the children's findings and their implications can be compared with similar details from some years ago.

2 My teacher

Help the children to create a profile of you. Be prepared for some criticism as well as praise! Let the children do a life-drawing of you in a typical outfit and write about what you do and say in class. Set these alongside some descriptions of teachers in the past and old photographs. Create a display for the children to inspect and comment on.

Copymaster 30 is for the children to create their teacher 'portrait'.

3 Other people I meet in school

Create profiles of the caretaker, the school cook, the cleaner, the ancillary, and other people who help in school. Use your judgement about who would be suitable people to draw, talk to and talk about. Work out a complete staff list with the children, and annotate it with some of the tasks these people do. Display it as an information sheet and the starting point for a discussion.

If the school has an archive of school records this should provide information about people employed there in the past. When compared with who works in the school now, the information will give some idea of changing views about staffing, dinners, and the growth of the school.

4 My school now

Help the children to discover some facts and figures about their school. For example, how many pupils, teachers, classrooms, buildings? **Copymaster 31** is a recording sheet for this activity.

5 A neighbouring school

Work with a teacher in a neighbouring school so that the children can make exchange visits and get information from each other. The neighbouring school may be different in size, location and accommodation. Before the visit, brief the children to make two or three comparisons between the neighbouring school and their own. You might like to split the class into groups to do this, so that each group is comparing two or three things. It is not essential that the children record anything during the visit, or they can record in pictures. However the novelty of sitting down in a 'strange' classroom will help to make any recording less of a chore.

The aim is to give the children the chance to compare two sets of information: the one about their own school and the comparison set about another (see below). Collate the information the children have accrued through the visit and, if they have not yet collected information about their own school to 'match' their findings, let them do so now, or when the children from the exchange school make their visit.

6 What I do in school

Talk with the children about the kinds of things they do in school. You could compile a list of what they say and then ask them, independently, to mark in order the three most important. This involves a key study skill; namely filtering the most important data from a mass and then prioritising that. Let the children draw and paint pictures of themselves in school. Annotate these

47

and add them to an existing display, or create one called 'What we do in school' (see above).

7 The name of my school

Show the children the full name of their school. If it is CP (County Primary) or CI (County Infant), explain that the school is looked after by the LEA (Local Education Authority). Tell the children where the offices for this authority are and what the people do in those offices. If the school is Voluntary Controlled, this means that the Church owns the buildings and occupies a minority of places on the governing body. If it is Voluntary Aided, the Church not only owns the buildings but forms a majority on the governing body and has a good deal of influence on how things are done. The importance of all this to the children and their study of history is two-fold. First, the name of their school should not be a mystery to them, and second, the name of the school may tell something about how the school came to be established in the first place.

8 What school is for

Basing your discussion on what the children have done already in this topic, but particularly on Activity 6, elicit the children's views about what school is for. They may say, for example, that school is for learning, to read, to write, to do sums, to do experiments, to play with friends, to work with other children. You will be able to draw out those purposes the children think most important, and later they will be able to compare these with what seem to have been the main purposes of schooling in the past. For example, many boys in medieval times would have been taught swordsmanship (there may be some who regard fighting as part of schooling now!); and schooling in the past was often more rooted in religion than it is now in most schools. Using the children's ideas, create a class statement about the purposes of schooling as they see them. This could be part of a whole-topic display or could even go into the school handbook.

9 My Mum and Dad at school

Ask the children to quiz their mum, dad or someone who looks after them about their own schooldays. Give the children clues about what to ask. For example:

What time did you set off for school?
How did you get there?
Did you wait on the playground? Was there a bell to go in? Did you have to line up?
What were the desks/teachers/books/classrooms like?
Was there a playtime?
Did you have school dinners? What were they like?
What happened if you did something naughty?
What happened if you did something especially good?
Tell me about your favourite teacher.
What did you dislike about school?

Copymaster 32 is a collection sheet for information about schooling. If you decide to make the collection 'formal' by sending home the copymaster, it will be necessary to send also a short note telling parents what you are doing with the children and why you would like their help. The children can write in the responses on the copymaster themselves if they are able to, or they can ask mum or dad to do the writing. For the very young it will be sufficient to ask them to draw one

222222

2222222

Mums and Dads at school

Proof! School photos	School rules	Being naughty	Good work	Uniform	Talking to Teacher
	There were bells for lessons, doors for boys and girls, silence in the dining hall.	Ellen's mum had to write 'I must not be rude to Miss Arkwright' 200 times! Tim's dad got the cane often.	There were prizes --- Book of Art. Natalie's Mum's prize and gold stars.	Peter's dad hated his cap and tie. Haircuts short!	Donald's dad called his teacher 'sir' and stood up to speak to him.

good and one bad thing the adult mentions about school. Back at school, you and the children will have fun sorting out what has been said. There will, of course, be a number of ways in which the information can be presented (one example is given above). Let the children offer some ideas about the kinds of memories to put together.

10 School for grandparents
As in Activity 9, the children can ask a grandparent, or someone elderly whom they know well, about schooldays in the past.

11 Old school reports and prizes
Young children may not yet use subject labels for their learning. This attitude is to be encouraged, so do not use this activity if it will destroy their 'openness'. Also, children may not find old documents of interest to them. However, if these issues don't arise, you can get hold of some old school reports or school prizes, perhaps your own or those belonging to relatives or colleagues, and show these to the children. Point out the things studied in school. At the time of publication the *Guardian* newspaper was printing extracts from school reports of people in the public eye, each week in the Friday edition.

12 School long ago
Assemble and display pictures and photographs of Victorian and Edwardian schoolrooms and schoolchildren. If you have some reproductions of paintings you could show these to the children. Take some photographs of your own classroom and the children at work, and get a colleague to take a picture of you at work. Mount these and set them alongside the 'old' pictures (see opposite). Give the children magnifiers and let them look for and comment on the differences between the two sets.

13 School in stories
Find some story books about school (see those listed under *Resources*). Video some children's TV programmes showing schoolrooms and school scenes, for example episodes of *Simon and the Witch* and *Mr Majeika*.

Read some extracts aloud and let the children watch the video snippets.

Search out some descriptions of school and teachers in stories written long ago – Mr Gradgrind in Dickens' *Hard Times* is pretty formidable. Also, autobiographies may yield schooltime memories, for example Edith Nesbit's *Long ago when I was young* tells of her distress about her arithmetic. Have an oral review in which the children comment on what they have heard in stories and seen on video.

Copymaster 33 invites the children to comment on the realism of a school in a story they have read when compared with their own school.

14 Schoolbooks
Instructional books for children that were written not too long ago sometimes seem quaint in style and presentation. There may also be at the back of a cupboard in school, some old reading-scheme books and information books. Show some of these old schoolbooks to the children and let them comment on the differences between these and the books they currently use.

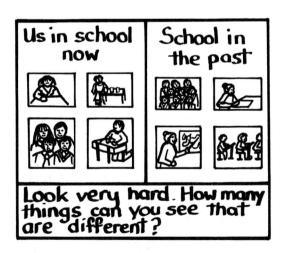
Us in school now / School in the past
Look very hard. How many things can you see that are different?

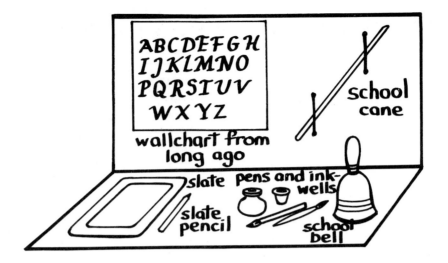

15 School equipment old and modern

Add to Activity 14 by introducing some old school equipment, for example, a slate and slate-pencil, a dip-in pen, an inkwell, an old alphabet chart, an old school bell (which may still be in use) and, if one can be found, a cane. Attach the cane firmly to the display so that none of the children are tempted to try it out (see above). Act as a 'guide' to show the children the display and answer their questions about the things there. Make sure, by pretend demonstration, that they know how the things were used. Leave the things on display so that the children can handle them (except for the cane!).

Copymaster 34 shows pictures of a modern school-room and a Victorian schoolroom, which the children can compare.

16 School clothes

Talk to the children about the kinds of clothes they wear to school. Your school may have a uniform. Display some items of clothing alongside pictures of their friends that the children have drawn. Annotate these to focus on what the children are wearing. Add to the display some old photographs which show what

children wore to school in years gone by (see below). Family photograph albums may yield suitable pictures so, if it is appropriate, you could send a short note to parents about this topic and ask if they have any photographs they can lend.

Copymaster 35 invites the children to compare pictures of schoolchildren now and in Edwardian times. They can compare the clothes for style, materials, likely comfort and ease of movement.

17 Cheeky school rhymes

Children love the idea of being irreverent about school and rhymes like the following are winners:

We break up, we break up, we don't care if the school blows up.

No more English, no more French, no more sitting on the old school bench.

Look with the children at the wording of these. For example, the reference to 'the old school bench' can tell children something of school in days gone by. Make a class rhyme book for the book corner; it will be read until dog-eared.

50

EXTENSION ACTIVITIES

1 The story of my school

This investigation may have begun in Activity 4. As an extension, a thorough examination of school records, any relevant county records, and old newspaper clippings should yield a portrait of the school and its history.

2 'Old' pupils

Using old registers, the children's family information and local knowledge, help the children to trace some former pupils of the school who still live locally. Then help the children to compose a letter asking if these people are willing to talk about their memories of the school. In response to favourable replies let the children, accompanied by a teacher, visit the ex-pupils and ask them a few questions, or invite them to come into school to talk to the children. Record, collate and discuss the information gained.

3 School in comics

Buy one issue of each of the comics intended for children under nine. Let the children look for all the references to school and stories about school and critically review them. Mount the relevant pages of the comics, annotated with the children's remarks. If possible, try to get hold of some really old comics. If appropriate, expose them to similar analysis but keep them safe and intact. Compare the results.

4 Teachers' own schooldays

Arrange for the children, with your help, to interview all the teachers in the school, asking them about their own schooldays. Keep it simple, with just three or four questions. Here are some suggestions:

Did you enjoy school most of the time?
Tell us three things you enjoyed/did not enjoy about school.
Tell us about one of your teachers.
Did you ever get the cane or slipper? (If yes) Tell us why. (If no) Tell us about one of the times you got told off.

To avoid having to write down all the replies, the children could either tape-record the interview or come straight back to the class and report their findings orally. You, the teacher, can then be scribe and write down their discoveries. **Copymaster 32** can be used again here to record the findings.

Topic: School. Suggested level(s) of work involved in activities

Core Activity Number	Level	Core Activity Number	Level	Extension Activity Number	Level
1	1/2	10	2/3	1	3
2	1/2	11	2/3	2	3
3	1/2	12	2/3	3	3
4	2	13	2/3	4	3
5	2/3	14	2/3		
6	1/2	15	2/3		
7	2	16	2/3		
8	2/3	17	2/3		
9	2/3				

BEING A CHILD

TOPIC WEB

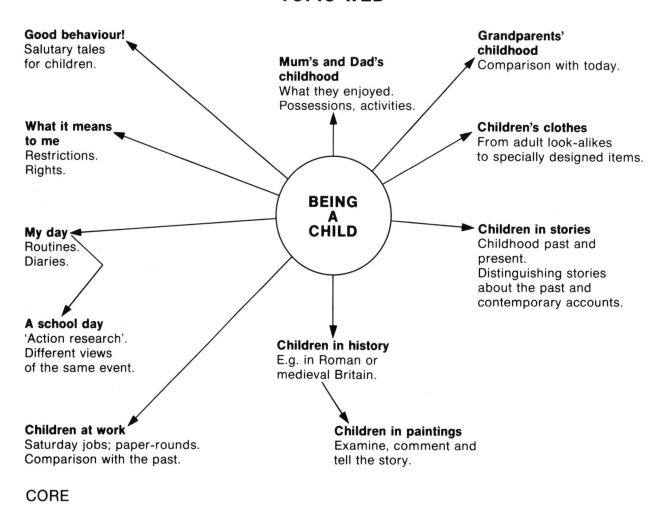

Good behaviour!
Salutary tales
for children.

Mum's and Dad's childhood
What they enjoyed.
Possessions, activities.

Grandparents' childhood
Comparison with today.

What it means to me
Restrictions.
Rights.

Children's clothes
From adult look-alikes
to specially designed items.

BEING A CHILD

My day
Routines.
Diaries.

Children in stories
Childhood past and
present.
Distinguishing stories
about the past and
contemporary accounts.

A school day
'Action research'.
Different views
of the same event.

Children in history
E.g. in Roman or
medieval Britain.

Children at work
Saturday jobs; paper-rounds.
Comparison with the past.

Children in paintings
Examine, comment and
tell the story.

CORE

EXTENSIONS

Poems and sayings
Collecting and
finding origins.

Babies and baby care
Now and in the past.
Equipment.
Customs.

Children's needs
Own needs compared
with UN Convention
on the Rights of the
Child.

THIS TOPIC AND THE NATIONAL CURRICULUM ▶

Work in this topic can be treated as part of a broader cross-curriculum theme with links including the following:

English   All aspects
Mathematics   Calendars, ages and birthdays
Science   Growth and size
Technology   Effects of machines on our lives

Geography   Childhood in other nations and cultures
Creative arts
— *Art*   self-portraits
— *Drama*   playlets and stories about children

ABOUT THIS TOPIC ▶

General points

● As with the topic *Family*, this topic demands your sensitivity. Ideas about children and childhood vary from one family to another and within and across cultures. The children need to understand that rules in other families may be different from those in their own, but are no less correct. You must also be sensitive to the needs of children and adults in families, and not intrude on the privacy of family life.

Childcare in history

The ways in which children and childhood have been viewed is reflected in the ideas about childcare that prevailed in the past. Until about the 1400s children were not thought to need to be close to parents physically or emotionally. Wet-nurses, beatings, infanticide and emotional coldness were the order of the day. It was common for children to be fostered with another family, while parents in their turn received children from a different household.

From the 14th to the 17th century children were still viewed as the possession and property of their parents and ripe for 'physical moulding'. It was during this period that child-instruction manuals arrived and motherhood began to mean closeness to children, but emphasis was still placed on children's obligations to their parents rather than parents' responsibilities to their children.

In the eighteenth century, parents began to feel they could affect a child's mind as well as body. Children were nursed by their mothers, not swaddled, taught to pray, smacked rather than whipped, and made to obey with threats of punishment.

It is really only during the nineteenth century that children came to be seen as having any distinctive place in the world, other than as 'small adults' or as the possessions of their parents. From the 1800s to the middle of this century training, teaching and socialising became the accepted pattern of care; sometimes harsh discipline was meted out. Fathers began to have the chance to take a more active part in children's lives.

Currently, some people are beginning to see children as having individual needs and requirements, which both parents and teachers can help them to realise by the investment of considerable time and deliberate effort. The 'ideal' of some is that children should develop 'naturally'; they recognise that children have rights and parents responsibilities, and that adults should try to be empathic with children's feelings and views.

Children at work

Eight hundred years ago even very young children helped the family income by, for example, gathering nuts and berries and collecting tufts of sheep-wool. When slightly older they would herd geese and pigs and snare rabbits, and by the age of ten would be full workers. Carding, spinning and weaving of wool were cottage industries for hundreds of years, and children helped with these.

Agricultural reform, including enclosure acts and the introduction of machinery, forced people to move from rural to urban life. Women and children who had worked at home were employed in mills and factories. In the 18th century when, with urban development, houses were built higher and chimneys became narrower and taller, small destitute and poor boys were made to scrabble up to scrape away the soot. This practice carried on until the next century, despite the introduction of chimney brushes and the health risk to the children.

RESOURCES ▶

Artefacts
Obtain childhood belongings and clothes from the children themselves, from adult relatives, from the Museum Service and other sources.

Pictures and photographs
These should be of children now and in the past and include some reproductions of famous paintings. Here are some examples:

Chardin *Girl with battledore*
      Morning toilet
      Saying grace
Denning *Queen Victoria at the age of four*
Gainsborough *Cottage Children*
Millais *The boyhood of Raleigh*

Velasquez *Prince Philip Prosper of Spain*, c. 1660
Watteau *The dance*
Yeames *And when did you last see your father?*

Story books

Ahlberg, A. *Here are the Brick Street Boys*; *A Place to Play*; and *Fred's Dream*, Collins/Picture Lions.
Ahlberg, J. and A. *The Baby's Catalogue*, Kestrel/Picture Puffin.
Blanco, J. and D'Ham, C. *Anna Then and Anna Now*, Young Library.
Brisley, J. L. *The Milly Molly Mandy Books*, Harrap/Puffin.
Cleary, B. *The Ramona Books*, Puffin.
Colwell, E. *Bad Boys*, Puffin.

Dahl, R. *Charlie and the Chocolate Factory*, Puffin.
Edwards, D. *My Naughty Little Sister*, Magnet.
Hoban, R. *Bedtime for Frances* and *Bread and Jam for Frances*, Faber and Faber/Scholastic.
Hoffman, H. *Struwwelpeter*, Forum Books.
King, C. *Stig of the Dump*, Puffin.
Lively, P. *A Stitch in Time*, Puffin.
McPhail, D. *Pig-Pig Grows Up*, Macmillan.
Miller, M. *What Size is Andy?*, Methuen.
Morgan, H. *Meet Mary Kate*, Puffin.
Nabb, M. *The Josie Smith Stories*, Collins/Young Lions.
Nesbit, E. *The Railway Children*; *Five Children and It*; *The Treasure Seekers*, Puffin Classics.

Richemont, E. *The Time Tree*, Walker Books.
Smith, P. *Jenny's Baby Brother*, Collins/Picture Lions
Sowter, N. *Maisie Middleton*, A & C Black/Picture Lions.
Thompson, K. *Eloise*, Puffin.
Walsh, J. P. *A Chance Child*, Puffin.

Information books

Merson, E. *et al.*, *Children in the War: Home and School in the 1950s*, Longman.
Steel, A. *Victorian Children*, 'Beginning History' series, Wayland.

CORE ACTIVITIES

C36 –40

1 Me: a child

Ask the children to talk about what it means to be a child. For example, they may say toys, going to bed early, being good, not doing as they like, not being able to choose or decide things. Let them record in pictures some of the things that they associate with themselves and childhood. **Copymaster 36** provides a record sheet.

2 My day

'Ourselves' is a regular subject for discussion in infant classrooms. Use one such discussion or 'news' time to get the children to describe a typical day. Chart the day of several children and set them alongside one another for comparison. This could be the first step in writing a diary and a starting point for comparison with the day of a child in another era. (See below.)

3 A school day

To take a critical look at a school day the children may need some practice in being aware of what is going on. Set aside one day as an 'action research' day. Throughout the day, which should otherwise be fairly ordinary, ask the children to note in single words or pictures what they are doing and what is 'going on'. They may note how they feel too. Assign a part of the day for you to annotate and collate their observations,

with their help. After the children have gone home, carefully examine their work, looking especially for different versions of the same event. On the following day ask the children to share their memories of what they did and how they felt about the day before. Show the children their comments, which you have summarized in a class book. By drawing the views together you should be able to show the children that, though they were all in the class and all spent the day together, as researchers or diarists they did not all view the day in the same way nor were their memories or interpretations similar. This is an important point in understanding and evaluating historical accounts.

4 My Mum/Dad as a child

Give the children a few ideas about things they can find out about their parents' childhood. For example, they could ask about a favourite outfit, best friends, outdoor games, what they did in the evenings and at weekends, how much pocket-money they had and what their favourite TV programmes were. Assemble the children's information into a picture and word display, or a portfolio of snippets about many mums and dads.

Copymaster 37 is a sheet of suggested questions for the children to ask their mum or dad, with room to record; and **Copymaster 38** enables children to make direct comparisons between themselves and their

mum or dad as a child. Copymaster 38 has been deliberately left open, with no suggestions or border, since you may wish the children to compare some specific aspects of children, like leisure or pocket-money or favourite comics and books.

5 My Gran/Grandad as a child
Ask the children to repeat the finding-out process they used in Activity 4, using questions that include some of their own. If it is feasible, it may be more appropriate to invite to school a gran or grandad whom you know well, so that they can face an audience of several child interviewers. An extended profile of this particular visitor's childhood can be built up as a result of the questioning, and perhaps some toys and clothes of the right age can be set alongside it on display.

If finding a gran to talk to the children is difficult, there may be an older person in the local community who, though nobody's gran, is of the right age and is able to talk to small children easily.

6 Children in stories
Choose a few stories which describe how childhood is now and was in the past. Read some passages to the children and discuss the differences. For example, you could include extracts from *Josie Smith*, *Oliver Twist*, *The Water Babies*, *Stig of the Dump* and *The Treasure*

Seekers. Let the children compare their childhood with one story-book account and, on folded card, draw a 'now' picture on the right and a 'past' picture on the left. Write a caption to emphasise the contrast.

7 Stories past and present
Look at some stories about children and try to establish when each was written. Was the author writing about a time that was already in the past or about children at the time when the book was written? You could include the stories mentioned in Activity 6. Show the children how they can establish when the stories were first published and hence discover whether, when they were written, they were contemporary accounts or about the past. For example, much of Dickens' work is social comment about life at the time as well as good narrative, and the things the Bastable children say in Edith Nesbit's books are contemporary with the time of original publication. In *The Time Tree* E. Richemont writes about girls now and long ago. Accounts of how children behaved in the past make good starting points for discussion.

8 Children in recent history
Using information gleaned in earlier activities in this topic, let the children set out what they know on a timeline (see below). For example, their gran may have gone to Saturday morning pictures until she was in her teens, and now children watch Saturday morning television.

Copymaster 39 invites children to record in pictures children from their great grandparents', grandparents' and parents' time. For example, they may want to show working children, children listening to the radio, and children watching a video or riding bikes.

9 Childhood in an historical setting

Choose an era in history and help the children investigate what the life of a child might have been like. For example, you might choose Roman Britain and look at the lives of British children, or of the Roman children in Britain; or choose the life of the son of a medieval merchant or of a servant in a castle following the Norman conquest. This needs careful researching on your part to assemble resources beforehand. Artefacts or replicas and picture-books will help the children to begin to understand what life as a child may have been like long ago.

10 Children and work

Investigate and discuss the rules about children and work nowadays. Find out whether any of the children have brothers, sister or other relatives who do Saturday work or a paper-round. Explain to the children that, long ago, most children did not have 'free time' as we know it, and tell them about the kinds of work that youngsters did, including factory work and farmwork and cleaning chimneys. Display 'jobs' children do nowadays and work children did in the past (see examples illustrated below).

11 Children and clothes

Some of the activities in the topic *Clothes* can be borrowed or adapted to use in this topic. With the children's help, assemble a collection of children's clothes, past and present. Ask the children whether there are things at home that were worn by their mum/dad or grandparents when little, that may be brought to school. Use the Museum Service and Library Service to supply clothes and pictures of children from long ago. In the light of what you have collected examine a particular aspect of dress; and discuss also the transition in children's clothing (largely this century) from imitation-adult to 'designer' fashion.

12 Children in paintings

There are some very famous paintings which depict children (see the list under *Resources*). Provide reproductions of some of these and discuss what the children are doing, how they may be feeling, and what the story of each picture is.

13 Behaving yourself!

The book *Struwwelpeter* is full of salutary tales about children and some of the dangers they face. The children could write or draw, for fun but in the *Struwwelpeter* fashion, what they think might happen if they watch too much TV or chew gum or stay up late. There is some element of threat in other stories and poems too. For example, the characters who feature in Roald Dahl's *Charlie and the Chocolate Factory* are pretty gruesome, and poems by Ogden Nash and Hilaire Belloc can add to the list of fates befalling 'naughty' boys and girls. This activity could be related to a discussion of the standards of behaviour expected of children now, and the real situations of danger for children in Britain today, which, in turn, could lead into how the children can help themselves to stay safe. For example, in addition to the threat of Harriet and the matches, which is just as potent today as ever, you can talk about road safety, stranger-danger and a healthy diet.

Copymaster 40 is designed to help children invent their own comic-strip 'salutary tale'.

Children at work: In the fields / In the factories / In the kitchens / Doing a Saturday job / Doing a paper-round

EXTENSION ACTIVITIES

1 Babies now

Let the children research some of the things mothers commonly have for a new baby. There may be a mum of one of the children who has recently had a baby, who will tell the children about disposable nappies, Babygros®, sterilising units, cots and buggies. Assemble a display of some of the things a modern baby is said to need.

2 Babies then

Encourage the children to find out all they can about the treatment of babies in times past, and offer it as a comparison with babycare nowadays. For example, they may discover about children being tied to a board and hung up!, swaddled, or dressed in layer upon layer of clothing.

3 Sayings and poems about children

Help the children to assemble a collection of sayings and poems about children and babies. For example, the sayings might include: 'Children should be seen and not heard'; 'Spare the rod and spoil the child'. They could trace the origins of these and discuss their implications for changing attitudes to children.

4 Children's needs

This is rather a sophisticated investigation and will prove a challenge to good researchers! Let the children ask some of their classmates what children need. This may yield information like 'home, clothes, love, toys'. They can collate this information, and then see if they can find any evidence that what today's children think are basic needs have been denied to children at any time in the past. Finally, they could examine extracts from the United Nations Convention on the Rights of the Child to see whether it matches their classmates' declared needs.

Topic: Being a child. Suggested level(s) of work involved in activities

Core Activity Number	Level	Core Activity Number	Level	Extension Activity Number	Level
1	1	8	2/3	1	1
2	1	9	3	2	1/2
3	2	10	2/3	3	2/3
4	2/3	11	2/3	4	3
5	2/3	12	2/3		
6	2/3	13	3		
7	2/3				

FOOD AND COOKING

TOPIC WEB

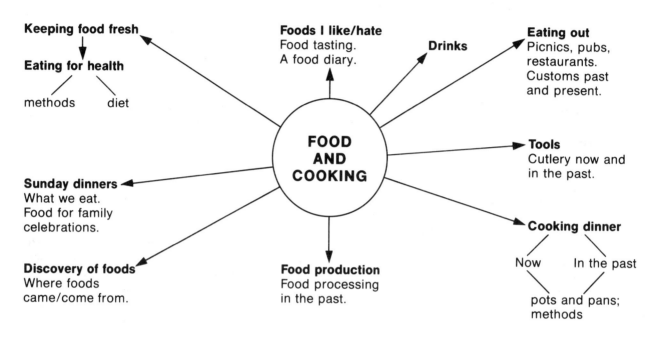

Keeping food fresh

Eating for health

methods   diet

Foods I like/hate
Food tasting.
A food diary.

Drinks

Eating out
Picnics, pubs,
restaurants.
Customs past
and present.

**FOOD
AND
COOKING**

Tools
Cutlery now and
in the past.

Sunday dinners
What we eat.
Food for family
celebrations.

Cooking dinner

Now   In the past

pots and pans;
methods

Discovery of foods
Where foods
came/come from.

Food production
Food processing
in the past.

CORE

EXTENSIONS

A big 'spread'
Medieval feasts.
Samuel Pepys'
dinner party.
A Victorian
family dinner.

**Origins of
'food' words**

**Origins of
famous foods**
Regional delicacies.

Convenience foods
What are they?
Why do we have them.

THIS TOPIC AND THE NATIONAL CURRICULUM ▶

Work in this topic can be treated as part of a broader cross-curriculum theme with links including the following:

English   All aspects
Mathematics   Weighing and measuring in cooking;
   interpreting recipes; portion size and fractions
Science   Making cakes and bread rise; mixtures
   and compounds; change of state
Technology   Design for a purpose, for example, pans
   and cups
Geography   Food sources round the world; recipes
   from different countries

Creative arts
— *Art*   'still life'; playdough food
— *Drama*   healthy eating; 'the story of bread' and
   stories and rhymes like *Have you seen the Muffin
   Man?*
Health Education   eating for healthy body and
   sound teeth

ABOUT THIS TOPIC ▶

General points

● Foods relished within one culture may not be so in others. If in your class you are lucky enough to have children from a variety of cultures, this is a topic in which you can capitalize on that wealth of experience and make it part of everyone's learning.

Food and drink in history

Cooking in a cottage in Norman times was done in a single pot over the fire. Most of the time the pot contained only vegetables. When meat was available it was usually pork. Pigs were economical to keep because they were good scavengers and virtually every part of the carcase could be put to good use. Those living in castles had the advantage of storage space so salted and smoked food could be laid up for winter or against siege. Salt was expensive and a valuable commodity, stored in a special niche near the fire. Scurvy was rife in winter among the poor; only those who were better off avoided it because they had a more varied diet. Deer, wild boar, hare, fish, and doves from the dovecote featured in the meals of the wealthy, and a cow could be fed all winter to provide fresh milk.

In medieval times people began to eat butter rather than use it merely for medicinal and cooking purposes.

Cheeses were not distinguished by name, but simply called 'soft' or 'hard'. Potatoes did not arrive until the reign of Elizabeth I. Samuel Pepys, writing in the second half of the seventeenth century, sets out the menu for a dinner party he gave for six guests, himself and his wife. They ate oysters, a hash of rabbits, a lamb, and a rare chine of beef, and then roasted fowl, tart and cheese. All that cost nearly £5!

The invention of the kitchen range in 1780 meant that a housewife could air clothes, cook food and boil water, and use an oven – all more economically than before. The only drawback was its nearness to the floor, so that it was necessary to lift and stoop.

Mrs Beeton's cookery book was first published in 1861 and it is still in print today, in updated editions. The book amply demonstrates the kinds of foods enjoyed by some people in Victorian times. It was in Victorian times that housewives first benefited from canned food including, by 1890, meat, fish, vegetables and fruit; and from margarine, and meat and fish imported in refrigerated ships.

During World War II there was food rationing. Extra milk was available for pregnant and nursing mothers, and orange juice and cod-liver oil for children. House-wives were advised to try baking cakes without butter or sugar and pies without meat or fruit in order to overcome shortages of certain foods.

RESOURCES ▶

Artefacts
Provide a variety of kitchen pots and tools, including the equipment to make bread or cheese in school, and a collection of cutlery.

Pictures
Collect pictures of a variety of kitchens and cooking arrangements through the centuries.

Information
Supply a variety of food wrappings and packaging showing the country of origin; a globe or a world map.

Story books
There seem to be few stories in print which focus on food in the past but any story about food can be used to start up the discussion. Here are a few suggestions:

Clarke, D. *Shepherd's Pie,* Julia McRae/Hippo.
Crossland, C. *Patrick's Perfect Pancake,* Walker Books.
Demarest, C. L. *No Peas for Nellie,* Picturemac.
De Paola, T. *The Magic Pasta Pot,* Andersen Press.
Ehlert, L. *Growing Vegetable Soup,* Gollancz.
Garland, S. *Having a Picnic,* The Bodley Head.

Hoban, R. *Dinner at Alberta's,* Cape.
Lord, J. V. *The Giant Jam Sandwich,* Piccolo.
Macdonald, E. *Miss Poppy and the Honey Cake,* Aurum Books.
Rogers, P. *Lily's Picnic,* The Bodley Head.
Thwaite, A. *A Piece of Parkin,* Andre Deutsch.

Information books
Chaney, L. *Breakfast* from the 'Turn of the Century' series, A & C Black.
Cobb, V. *Feeding Yourself,* Hodder and Stoughton.
Davies, K. and Oldfield, W. *Food,* Wayland.
Deshpande, C. *Finger Foods* from the 'Friends' series, A & C Black.
Illsley L., *Cheese* from the series 'Food', Wayland.
Lawrie, J. *Pot Luck: Cooking and Recipes from the Past,* A & C Black.
Sproule, A. *British Food and Drink,* and others in the series 'Food and Drink', Wayland.
Solomon, J. *Chopsticks and Chips* from 'The Way We Live' series, Hamish Hamilton.
Steele, P. *Food and Drink,* Heinemann.

CORE ACTIVITIES

1 My favourite foods
Share with the children your list of favourite foods. Let them record in words or pictures their favourite foods and report the results to the whole class. Compile a chart of 'all-time' favourites and let the children paint, draw and do collage pictures of themselves eating these foods. **Copymaster 41** invites the children to draw or write about some of their favourites.

2 Food tasting
Ask several parents to help you supply a range of foods the children can pick up and try in school. They do not have to be typically 'British' foods, in fact the wider the range the better. Make sure no foods are included that some children should not try because of their religion or their parents' views. Let the children try the foods (having washed their hands first). They can then do a 'taste and tell' recording activity, judging taste, texture and colour, and giving each food a star rating. Up to three stars is probably enough: one for 'do not like', two for 'quite like' and three for 'like a lot'. **Copymaster 42** is a food-tasting rating sheet.

3 Food day-diary
Ask the children to write down all that they ate and drank yesterday. This information could be made into a book for the story corner.

It could also be put onto a database for comparison with information about other children in the school, with what adults ate when they were young, or with the same age group in subsequent years.

4 Sunday dinners
Compile a composite 'Sunday dinner' (or Saturday, or whenever a special meal is eaten in the week). You may arrive at a grand mixture of food, depending on the eating habits of the families of the children in the class. Discuss the parts of the meal that are similar for everyone. For example, does everyone have savoury things first and sweet things afterwards? Does everyone have a 'staple' food like bread, potatoes or rice? Create a display showing the things we eat for 'Sunday dinner' (see opposite).

5 Family celebrations and food
Discuss the foods that families always have at celebration meals. This activity is an attempt to get the children thinking about traditions in families and it

may overlap with Activity 4 above. Introduce children to the idea that some foods are associated with being English or Welsh. You could mention, for example, roast beef, Yorkshire pudding, 'English' breakfast, Welsh cakes, laver 'bread' and fish and chips. Introduce information about other cultures, including all those represented in your class.

6 Foods I hate
Discuss with the children the foods they dislike and why. Help them to display this information in a variety of ways, including, for example, a bar-chart, and with artificial foods made from junk materials.

7 How Mum or Dad cooks the dinner
Talk to the children about the cooking arrangements in their houses. They may all use electricity or gas; there may be children whose families have solid-fuel cookers; the kitchen may be shared. Remind the children of the dangers of cookers, flames and matches. As a group, look at a variety of pictures of contemporary cooking appliances, and then use advertising brochures (e.g. from gas and electricity showrooms) to add to pictures the children themselves produce. Find out how the gas and electricity supplies reach the children's homes. Display the pictures alongside the outcomes of Activity 8, below.

60

8 How dinners were cooked long ago
Discuss the ways in which food can be cooked without modern appliances. Look at pictures of food being cooked over fires and on kitchen ranges and show the children how a spit works. Let them make model fires showing how people long ago cooked food outside, in the centre of the house, in a fireplace set in a wall and on a kitchen range. Display these models with some appropriately dressed dolls tending them (above).

Copymaster 43 shows some pictures of people cooking food in the past, that the children can put in a timeline and use as the basis for discussion. Top left is a Victorian range; top right a fireplace in a wall as used in the Middle Ages; bottom left a Viking dwelling (the smoke escaped through a hole in the thatched roof); and bottom right a large open fireplace with a spit, typical of large houses in the eighteenth century.

9 Food discovery in history
Investigate the diets of different classes in Britain before the discovery of the 'new world'. Find out what people ate before they had things like potatoes, tea and chocolate. Tell the story of Walter Raleigh's journeys.

10 Where our food comes from
With the children's help, assemble a collection of wrappings and labels from a wide variety of foods available to us. Using a globe or world map sort the labels into sets, according to country of origin. Mount the labels, making sure it is clear what kind of food each came from.

11 Food production long ago
Look with the children at the small-scale production methods used to make butter, cheese, bread and other foods in the past. Examine pictures of the kinds of implements used for this work, or better still, get hold of butter-pats, a bread-crock and a cheese-muslin to show the children. If the school is near a home where butter and cheese are still made on a small scale, find out whether the children may visit. Make some bread, butter and cheese in school. There are books available with instructions that the children can understand; for example there is a recipe for cheese-making in *Cheese* by Linda Illsley (see the information books list under *Resources*).

12 Cutlery past and present
Collect a range of cutlery, including a shaped baby-spoon and blunt knives, forks and spoons of a variety of styles and sizes. Talk with the children about what we use these utensils for. Let them say which foods they eat with their fingers, on a fork or spoon, and what they use a knife for. Explain that customs have changed over centuries. 'Pushers', for a baby to use, were popular at one time and forks were not used to eat with several hundred years ago. **Copymaster 44** gives children an opportunity to draw and write about cutlery now and in the past.

13 Cooking pots past and present
Make a collection of 'cooking pots and pans', ranging from pictures of ancient ones unearthed by archaeolo-

61

gists to, for example, Pearson's brown earthenware, decorated pottery, Pyrex, Le Creuset enamelled ironware, and non-stick. Discuss the relative merits of these pots, in shape and design and in the material they are made from. Find out how pottery is made.

14 Keeping food fresh

Nowadays many people can eat out-of-season food because we employ a variety of food-preservation methods. Find out what the children know about ways of keeping food fresh. Tell them about the methods used by people from ancient times, including salting and smoking. Then explain bottling, canning and freezing. Discuss the importance of preserving food in the past to provide winter stores and to offset bad harvests.

15 Food and health

Explain the importance of a balanced diet that includes foods from all the main food groups. Poor people still have impoverished diets. In the past many people failed to get essential nutrients and were therefore susceptible to scurvy and other deficiency diseases. Look at the problems of getting a range of foods in winter in the past, and the restricted range of foods available to the poor in, for example, Tudor or Victorian times.

16 Eating out: picnics, pubs and restaurants

Talk about picnics and have a class picnic lunch. Enlist the help of some parent volunteers by sending a letter to all parents explaining what your plans are and why. Set up the picnic for one lunchtime in the classroom, on the playing field or in the park. Discuss and draw what was eaten. Then, for comparison, discuss and draw what workers or children might have eaten as a picnic lunch in, say, medieval times and Victorian times (see above).

Check that the children know what a public house and a restaurant are. Discuss what a pub looks like, what is sold there, why the local one is so named and find out about its history. Tell the children about coaching inns and their importance as resting places for travellers and horses. Talk about the range of restaurants in Britain now which give us all a chance to eat foods and try recipes not available in the past.

17 Cafes in the classroom

Treat each corner of the room as an eating house from a different period in the past. You can create this setting over a period of time, perhaps tackling first a Georgian coffee-house or coaching inn, then an 'old-fashioned' formal restaurant, then a Chinese restaurant and finally a McDonald's. Discuss the likely differences in decor, clientele and food served. Then help the children to place these restaurants on a timeline (see below), with approximate dates for their introduction.

18 Drinks

During some of the other activities you may have talked about the range of drinks available. Draw together the likes and dislikes of the children, what they say their parents like, and other drinks available.

Decide what people drink most and compare this with the drinks available in other times. For example, though many of us drink tea a good deal now, tea was unknown in Britain until the 17th century.

EXTENSION ACTIVITIES

C45

1 A medieval feast

Do some research to discover what might have been eaten at a celebration meal many centuries ago. How would the food have been obtained, cooked and served? Who would have eaten the food? How would they have eaten it? What did the servants eat? Let the children make replica food, dress up in period costume, listen to period music, and re-enact a medieval 'party'.

Model food for our long ago feast.

2 Samuel Pepys and food

Search out extracts from Pepys' diary that tell us the kinds of things he enjoyed eating. Let the children list and collate these, and also copy some short extracts into a class book entitled 'Samuel Pepys and Food'. Make sure that the children can place Pepys in time. Then invite them to attempt a contemporary piece of writing, to 'match' an entry from Pepys' diary, about a party they went to or a meal they had recently.

3 A Victorian family dinner

Help the children in a library search for information about what Victorians liked to eat if they could afford good food. Jo Lawrie's book *Pot Luck* is a good resource to start with. Re-create a family dinner in pictures, which you could display as a 'flap' picture, with details of the recipes or how the food was eaten under each flap.

Using **Copymaster 45,** make a 'dinner through the ages' book. Ask the children to draw and name some suitable foods on each table and then cut the table strips apart. Help them to staple the strips together at the left-hand side. Open the book to view the food!

4 Where food words come from

Help the children to find out where some of the names we give to food and use about food come from. For example, 'dessert' comes from the French 'desservir' which means to clear away the dishes (it must be done before the pud!); a 'buffet' was a side shelf which dropped into use with a 'bang'; and a banquet was originally the name for a snack! You will need to consult a really good dictionary that explains word origins (there should be one in the public library).

5 The story of famous foods

Let the children write to manufacturers and producers of 'foods with a story', asking for information about the history of the food. The Tea Council in London and the Farmhouse Cheese Bureau in Wells, Somerset are two possibilities. You could also visit an 'exclusive' grocer's shop and study some of the food packaging, to get some ideas about which foods to investigate. Regional specialities like Cornish pasties, Bakewell pudding and Yorkshire parkin also have stories attached, which may merit investigation.

6 What is 'convenience food'?

Look at recent additions to the range of food available to us, including microwave dishes, complete meals and foods that are ready-prepared. Discuss why convenience foods are so-called, and why we are thought to need them nowadays.

A Victorian family dinner
Lift flaps to find out how the food is cooked.

63

Topic: Food and cooking. Suggested level(s) of work involved in activities

Core Activity Number	Level	Core Activity Number	Level	Extension Activity Number	Level
1	1	10	2/3	1	3
2	1	11	2/3	2	3
3	1/2	12	3	3	3
4	1/2	13	2/3	4	3
5	1/2	14	2/3	5	3
6	1/2	15	3	6	2/3
7	1/2	16	2/3		
8	2/3	17	3		
9	2/3	18	3		

TRANSPORT

TOPIC WEB

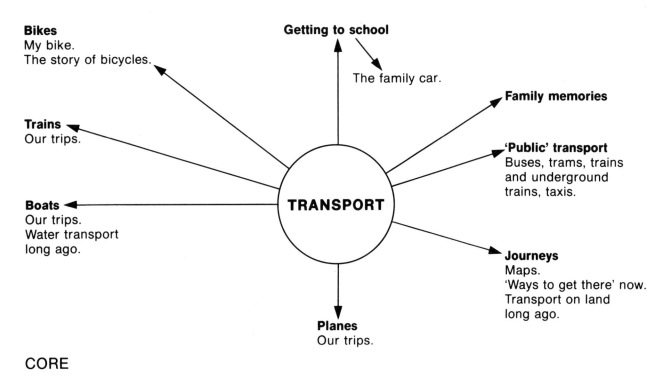

Bikes
My bike.
The story of bicycles.

Getting to school

The family car.

Trains
Our trips.

Boats
Our trips.
Water transport
long ago.

TRANSPORT

Planes
Our trips.

Family memories

'Public' transport
Buses, trams, trains
and underground
trains, taxis.

Journeys
Maps.
'Ways to get there' now.
Transport on land
long ago.

CORE

___

EXTENSIONS

The wheel
Practical models.
Discussion of the
importance of the
wheel.

Air transport
The story of flight.

Roads
History.
Construction.

**Maps and
transport**
Why roads, canals
and railways are
routed where they are.

Museum visit
Consolidation to topic.

Ships
The story of ships.

THIS TOPIC AND THE NATIONAL CURRICULUM ▶

Work in this topic can be treated as part of a broader cross-curriculum theme with links including the following:

English   All aspects
Mathematics   Time and distance
Science   Speed; sinking and floating
Technology   Wheels; transport design
Geography   Canals, rivers, roads, ports and airports;
   maps

Creative arts
— *Art*   drawing and painting different means of
   transport
— *Drama*   acting out stories of journeys

ABOUT THIS TOPIC ▶

General points

● This topic can begin, as usual, with the children themselves and their own experiences; and your starting point can also reflect the location of the school and its community. For example, if your school is in the heart of London you may choose to look at riverboats rather than transport on canals; if you work in Crewe, the railways and canals may be your focus.

● You are in the best position to decide whether a topic called 'transport' covering the whole gamut of people's efforts to get about, will be appealing to the children you teach; or whether they will find it more exciting to look at a journey they themselves could make easily and investigate how it might have been done at various times over thousands of years.

● While many children have experience of a wide variety of means of transport and go in the family car virtually every day, for others this will not be so, and you will need to tap into their likely experiences during discussion. We want to avoid branding children as affluent or poor as a result of discussions in class, and be just as sympathetic to the feelings of the child who has never ridden on the top of a bus but flies regularly on holiday, as to those who have rarely been in a car.

● There are some interesting dates and statistics about, for example, canal development and the number of passengers using the railways, in *The Longman Handbook of Modern British History 1714– 1987* by Chris Cook and John Stevenson.

Transport on land

The attempts of people to move themselves and their goods about, other than by walking and carrying what they could, have a very long history. By 5800 B.C. cattle were pulling loads along, and pull-along 'sledges' were used before wheels were invented. Horses were not used to pull loads for a long while after their domestication because they were thought to be much less efficient than oxen. With the adoption of the wheel (around 3000 B.C.), wagons and carts began to be developed, along with the idea of a road. It was the Romans who made their roads of a quality that enabled speedy communication and transport around their empire.

During the 15th century, vehicles that we know as coaches were devised. Passengers and the builders of these vehicles began to think of ways of making the ride less bumpy. Slings and springs to support carriages were introduced, and road surfaces were gradually improved. Well-drained roads with a curved surface, such as we have now, were introduced by people like Macadam in the early 1800s. Nowadays, motorway road surfaces are carefully laid to withstand the very heavy traffic.

In Britain people have paid to ride short distances in 'buses' for over a hundred years, for the first buses were horse drawn. In London, a bus service to carry 22 people ran from Paddington to Bank in 1829.

Steam-driven vehicles were used first on roads, but not very successfully, partly because road surfaces were poor. It was not until Trevithick, a British engineer who based his ideas on those already in use in the mining industry, had the idea of placing a steam-driven vehicle on continuous rails that the railway was born. The first in Britain ran from Stockton to Darlington in 1825.

Motor cars with internal combustion engines were the work of a Belgian, Lenoir, in 1863. Later in the century, Benz and Daimler further developed the idea of the automobile, first putting cars 'on the road', and then Henry Ford took a major role in making them widely available. In Britain in 1985 there were 16 453 000 private cars, and today many households have more than one.

Bicycles originally had no pedals. The first pedal-cycles had horse-like heads!

Water transport

For thousands of years people may have got around on water by sitting astride a log, or in a dugout canoe, with paddle or oar. We know that sails were used at least as early as 5000 B.C. Many nations used their seafaring skills to travel and conquer; for example, the Vikings.

Steamboats were first invented in the 17th century, and over the next one hundred and fifty years they were made increasingly reliable and fast and passenger liners were constructed. Brunel designed the *Great Western* (1838), which was the first steamship to cross the Atlantic regularly, and other famous ships including the *Great Britain* (1845) and the *Great Eastern* (1858).

Britain's canal system, begun in the middle of the eighteenth century, was an important inland means of transporting predominantly goods around industrial Britain.

Man in the air

This is truly a story of this century. Hot-air balloons had been in use since the late 18th century, but it was not until we had the internal combustion engine that the prospect of 'flying' became more than a dream. The key date is 1903, when the American Wright brothers got a powered flying machine airborne. The two World Wars speeded the technical advance of powered flight. The effects of air transport on our lives and our conception of the world are enormous. World travel is possible; we can write to relatives and friends in other parts of the world and letters arrive quickly; travel abroad is accessible to categories of people who, perhaps only one hundred years ago, would have spent their whole lives in and around their birthplace.

RESOURCES

Artefacts
Provide models of cars, boats and planes, preferably including some contemporary and some old ones.

Pictures
Include pictures of the development of the bicycle, car, boat and plane.

Information
You will need large-scale maps of the school and the streets around it, a map showing the location of the school in relation to the nearest big city and, if possible, a copy of an old map of the area around the school. Obtain timetables for local public transport services, whether bus, train or boat.

Story books
Curry, P. *The Big Red Bus Ride*, Picture Lions.
Lindall, F. *The Journey Home*, Walker Books.
Lippman, P. *Busy Boats and Busy Trains*, Random House.
McLean, A. and J. *The Steam Train Crew*, Oxford University Press.
Postgate, O. The *Ivor the Engine* books, Abelard Schuman/Picture Lions.
Walsh, J. P. *The Butty Boy*, Macmillan.

Information books
Bailey, D. *Planes and Cars* and *Trucks and Trains*, two titles in the series 'First Facts', Macmillan.
Butler, D. *Cars*, Simon and Schuster.
Dixon, M. *Land Transport* and *Flight* from the series 'Explaining Technology', Wayland.
Edom, H. *Living Long Ago: Travel and Transport*, Usborne.
Langley, A. *Let's Look at Bikes* from the 'Let's Look at' series, Wayland.
Lines, C. *Looking at Cars*, from the 'Looking at Transport' series, Wayland
Macdonald, F. and James, J. *A 19th Century Railway Station*, Simon and Schuster.
Macmillan Publishers *A New Look at Travel*.
Pace, C. and Birch, J. *Transport* from the 'Look Around You' series, Wayland.
Parker, S. *Flight and Flying Machines*, Dorling Kindersley.
Prince, R. *Railways*, Macdonald Educational.
Rickard, G. *Canals* from the 'Topics' series, Wayland.
Royston, A. *The Story of a Helicopter* from the 'On the move' series, Kingfisher.
Royston, A. *Just Look at Road Transport*, Macdonald Educational.
Scarry, R. *Cars and Trucks and Things that Go*, Collins.
Shone, V. *Wheels*, Orchard Books.

CORE ACTIVITIES

1 Getting to school
This is a starter activity to get children thinking about transport. The aim is to assemble some information which can be used to make comparisons with the past.

Ask the children how they get to school. If they all walk, you could ask them to time their journey one morning, with mum's or dad's help if necessary. If some come by car, they can explain why their parents choose this means of transport. Depending on the location of the school and the transport available to the children, you may also have bus or boat users in your class. This information can be collated in a variety of ways, including sets, block-graphs and on a database. If you wish, you can deliberately create data sets that you know will be empty, to fuel discussion. For example, 'On horseback' or 'By helicopter' are categories which may set the children thinking about some of the other choices of transport available or no longer available, and their limitations. Create a display of the data, which could include some toys and models to make the information more accessible.

2 The family car
If it is appropriate for the children you teach, find out who has a family car – some families may have more than one. List the makes and models, and display these

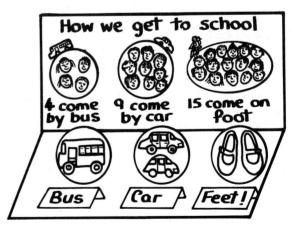

alongside advertising literature for cars. Make sets of cars that are the same in some way, for example, they are of the same colour, have two doors, or have more than two doors. Use criteria the children suggest to sort the vehicles. Find out the most popular make of car in use by the families and discuss what car ownership gives a family. One purpose of all this is to gather data against which to compare family memories about transport. Create a display or class book about the cars, or let each child create a book of their own. **Copymaster 46** gives the children a chance to record some facts about their family car.

3 Family memories

How did people in the children's families get about in the past? You could leave this information at an anecdotal level, by asking the children to ask their mums, dads and grandparents and having a discussion in school next day. Let the children paint pictures to tell the stories they have gleaned (see above).

If you want the children to attempt more detailed documentation, with their help prepare a short questionnaire that they can take home. Send an accompanying letter, explaining that you and the children are studying how people got around in years gone by. The resulting information will depend on the age of the respondents and where they have lived. **Copymaster 47** provides some starter questions that the children could ask of a number of adults.

4 My bike

If some of the children have bikes, let them tell their classmates about them. Ask the parents of one of the children if a bike can be brought into school for a day or two. Discuss how the bike works, how it has to be cared for and what its advantages are as a means of transport. Let the children paint pictures of the bike. Mention to the children that they are too young to ride on roads yet, but that they will (if appropriate) have the chance to take a cycling proficiency test when they are older. Start a display of paintings and information, which can be added to as a result of the next activity.

5 The story of bikes

Show the children pictures of the 'dandyhorse', 'penny-farthing' and other early bikes. Talk about the use of bikes to carry things around; for example, the letter post or newspapers may be carried in a bag on a bicycle. In towns, deliveries of bread and meat used to be made like this too. Display pictures of early bikes alongside those completed in Activity 4 (see below). If you have a group of children for whom bikes are especially fascinating, let them further explore the historical development of motorised bicycles and motorbikes.

6 What is 'public transport'?

Make sure the children understand what we mean by public transport, and talk about the services available in your area. How often can you get into the nearest town or city centre? How much are the fares? Find out how the fares have changed over a long period of time. What use do the children and their families make of the public transport system? Find out from the authorities how long these services have been running. Discuss with the children how they would travel if there was no public transport. If there is a good public transport service and it is one that is well used, the children may like to visit the depot, or main station, and talk to the manager about how the service works.

Copymaster 48 provides pictures of various kinds of road transport which, with your help, the children can put in a timeline, use for discussion, group into sets, and use as starting points for stories. Starting at the top left we have a sedan chair. This method of transport for the wealthy pre-dates the coach, extending from the use of litters in the Middle Ages to the specially made 'chairs' that were still for hire in London well into the eighteenth century.

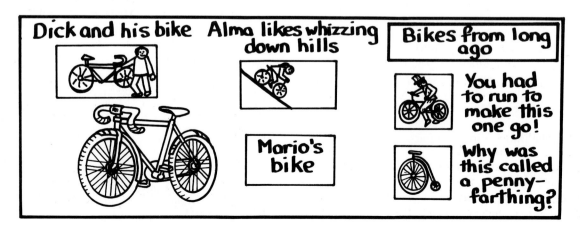

Stage-coaches probably started in Cromwell's time. The passengers slept each night at an inn along the route. Long-distance coaches became complicated pieces of machinery, the result of many years of development. The one shown is from the heyday of such coaches, around 1830. The fastest reached a speed of over 10 miles per hour but needed frequent changes of horses.

Trams were first used in the 1860s and were horse-drawn along fixed rails. Very soon, however, they were powered by electricity.

Motorcycles were introduced in 1885. The picture on the far left of the second row is of a powerful modern machine manufactured by Norton. Next to this is the Holden, one of Britain's first home-produced motor-cycles. It dates from 1895 and you can see its links with the bicycle.

The phaeton was a smart carriage for the rich, popular in Georgian times. They were comfortable, with good suspension.

On the third row, on the left, is a picture of a postboy from Stuart times, part of the Royal Mails system started by Charles I.

The penny-farthing was a type of bicycle that took its name from two British coins, because of the sizes of its wheels. The one shown is from about 1874.

The hansom cab was named after its inventor, Joseph Hansom. It was a light two-wheeled cab with a raised seat behind for the driver, a familiar sight in Victorian cities.

By 1914 horse-drawn buses and trams had disappeared in some large cities and had been replaced by vehicles powered by diesel engines. The bus illustrated is typical of the 1920s, having an open top deck.

The first railway in Britain was opened in 1825. The train shown here is of the type that ran on the new London–Birmingham railway in 1838.

The two cars featured are the Austin Mini, which reached great heights of popularity in the 1960s and today is becoming something of a collector's item; and the Ford Model T, popularly known as Tin Lizzie. Enormous numbers of the Ford were produced between 1908 and 1927.

7 Our train rides

Discuss the pleasures of a ride in a train. Let the children tell of their rail journeys, whether on miniature trains, steam-train pleasure trips, or Sprinters and Intercity trains. Discuss the speed of travel and where railways run, i.e. through hills, in valleys, through towns, near factories, etc. (See also Extension Activity 2.) It may be possible to take the children on a trainride locally, so that they can compare it with other forms of transport. Start a class book entitled 'Our trips by train, boat and plane'.

8 Our boat trips

How many children have been on a boat trip? Discuss the size of the boat, what powered it, where it took them, and how long the journey was. If it was a sea voyage, were any of the children ill? Tell them that Admiral Nelson never conquered his sea sickness! Add the children's pictures and anecdotes to the class book mentioned in Activity 7.

9 Our flights

Let those children who have been in an aeroplane discuss their experiences, and record them in a form suitable for the class book mentioned in Activity 7.

10 A look at a map

Let the children look first at a large-scale map showing the school and the streets immediately around it. Demonstrate to small groups how to position the map so that the streets are shown in positions that correspond with reality. Talk to the children about how a map is made, what a scale is, and how they can make judgements about distance using a map. Let them find out, using a few addresses from the register, who lives furthest away from school. Photocopy a part of the map and let the children mark in their own homes and their routes to school. Put some of these on display.

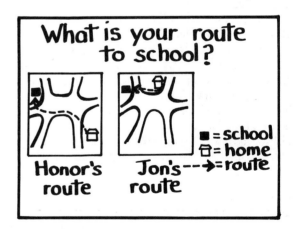

When the children can interpret the map, show them one on a smaller scale, preferably still including the school but also showing villages and the nearest town (or, if you are in a city school, the centre of the city). Talk about this map and how to use it. Make it a key resource in Activity 11.

11 Journeys we might make

Organise the children to work in groups and set them the challenge of making a journey from one location on the map to another. Ask them to think of as many possible ways as they can of reaching their goal. For example, you could show them that to travel by rail they must not only have a railway on that section of the map, but also stations where they can board and get off the train!

12 A journey long ago

Either using old maps of the area focused on in Activity 11, or old maps of another part of Britain altogether, discuss with the children how people might have travelled around long ago, and carried goods from one part of the land to another. Show them pictures of coaches, and people on horseback, and discuss the likely speed of travel and the problems associated with such journeys. Compare the journeys with those the children worked out in Activity 11.

13 Distances and signposts

Take the children to look at some signposts locally. Discuss what they mean and why they are important. If there are old stone sign blocks (milestones) at the side of the road, point these out to the children too. Using some of the distances the children have made a note of, help them to estimate the time it would take to travel that far using, say, a horse, a bicycle and a car. **Copymaster 49** invites the children to record work on signposts and distance.

14 Journeys by water long ago

Please do not study waterways unless the children can visit them, look at narrow-boats or river craft, or discover what a canal bridge or tug looks like.

Using the location of the school as a starting point, investigate with the children the local waterways or sea-transport systems. Local guides or someone interested in local history may be able to start a trail which enables children to discover facts about canals and their uses, or river and sea transport. Make a display of the findings, or combine them with those of a class of children further up the school to create a mixed-media presentation about one of the forms of transport. For example, the children could learn about the work lives and make models of life on the canals 100 years ago, and explore the related arts and crafts. With the help of a group of children through the primary age range you could set about recreating dramatically the life of canal folk. Stories like Jill Paton Walsh's *The Butty Boy* may provide inspiration.

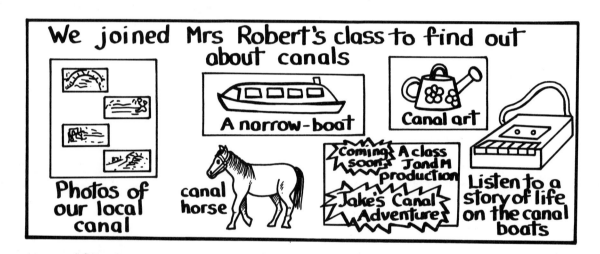

EXTENSION ACTIVITIES

C50

1 The wheel

This is intended as a practical exploration into the importance of the wheel. Explain to the children that there was a period of history when people did not know about the wheel. How would they have got about on land, and what did they use to carry things around? Supply the children with a range of junk-modelling materials, and construction materials like Lego® (without wheels), and ask them to invent things to get heavy loads from one place to another. They can, of course, include model animals in their ideas. Display their efforts and, in another session, let them use wheels as part of the construction. Display these results too. Discuss the apparent benefits of the wheel, judging by the models and the children's own observations. Add the discussion points to the display, alongside some pictures of 'pre-wheel vehicles' (but be careful not to show these to the children until they have finished with their own inventions).

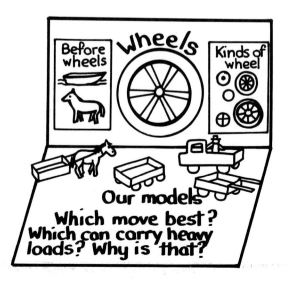

2 The story of roads

Investigate the story of roads and road builders of the past. Look at the importance of roads to the ancient Romans, and the developments in road surfacing. Ask if someone from the Highways Department or Motorway Maintenance Department is willing to show the children what makes up the surface of a road now, and what kinds of loads it is made to carry.

3 Maps and transport

Look at and compare new road maps with maps made some years ago of a sector of the country known to the children. Explore all the transport possibilities in the area, and discuss the likely reasons why the railways, canals and roads were routed in the way they have been. For example, canals can only be built uphill with systems of locks; trains cannot mount steep gradients and therefore have to go through tunnels or cuttings in hills.

4 Ships and other craft

Investigate the history of ships – to explore, carry things and to fight and conquer. Look at the development from very small boats to large ones manoeuvred with rudders and oars; and at the development of sailing ships, steamships and modern passenger liners. **Copymaster 50** invites children to create their own sequence of pictures, showing part of the story of ships.

5 Aeroplanes

Find out about the history of people and flight. This is an ideal project for an individual child capable of doing his or her own 'research'. The history of flight maps exactly onto the twentieth century, and there are many books which supply appropriate information at the right level. Model aircraft, including 'Airfix' models, could support this investigation.

6 Museum visit

There are specialist museums which would be of interest to children, either as a starting point for the Core Activities or (as I would favour) as a consolidation and 'bringing together' activity towards the end of the topic. Here are the names of some such museums:

Bath Carriage Museum
Boat Museum, Ellesmere Port
Crewe Heritage Centre
Hull Transport Museum
London Transport Museum, Covent Garden
Museum of Large Objects, Liverpool
National Railway Museum, York
Southampton Maritime Museum

Some general collections also have exhibits that are relevant, and it is worth finding out what is in the museums in your area.

Topic: Transport. Suggested level(s) of work involved in activities

Core Activity Number	Level	Core Activity Number	Level	Extension Activity Number	Level
1	1/2	8	1/2	1	1/2/3
2	1/2	9	1/2	2	3
3	1/2	10	2/3	3	3
4	1	11	3	4	3
5	1/2	12	3	5	3
6	2/3	13	3	6	1/2/3
7	1/2	14	3		

GOING TO WORK

TOPIC WEB

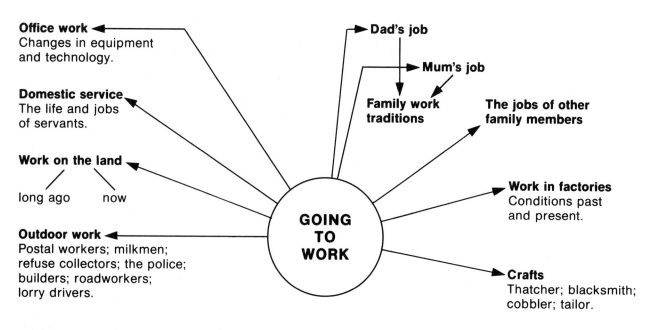

Office work
Changes in equipment
and technology.

Domestic service
The life and jobs
of servants.

Work on the land

long ago   now

Outdoor work
Postal workers; milkmen;
refuse collectors; the police;
builders; roadworkers;
lorry drivers.

Dad's job

Mum's job

**Family work
traditions**

**The jobs of other
family members**

**GOING
TO
WORK**

Work in factories
Conditions past
and present.

Crafts
Thatcher; blacksmith;
cobbler; tailor.

CORE

EXTENSIONS

**Study of an occupation
from the past**
An individual topic
related to the work of
a doctor, explorer,
nurse or sailor.

**Factory/museum
visit**
Visiting a modern
factory and an
industrial museum
to make
comparisons.

'Shadow' teacher
Children record
your day and
subsequently
discuss this
method of data
collection.

THIS TOPIC AND THE NATIONAL CURRICULUM

Work in this topic can be treated as part of a broader cross-curriculum theme with links including the following:

English   All aspects
Mathematics   Concepts of wages, salaries and shifts
Science   Industry and the environment, what makes
   machines 'go'
Technology   Raw materials to finished product, how
   things are made

Geography   Where industries were established and
   why
Creative arts
— *Art*   drawing and painting men and women at work
— *Drama*   mime (what's my job?); acting out episodes
   from people's work, for example 'people who help
   us', 'people who work while we sleep'

ABOUT THIS TOPIC ▶

General points

● This is another topic requiring sensitive treatment, for there may be children in your class who know about unemployment because their mum or dad is unemployed now, or whose parents struggle in two or three jobs to 'make ends meet'.

● Many people feel that a man has to have a job to maintain his dignity. This is despite the fact that, as the developed world moves into what is sometimes called the 'post-industrial' society, we may be facing a trend towards less than full employment, in the sense that it has been understood in the past. Notions about the importance of work have far-reaching effects on children. Not only do they affect the ways in which we and they view our history, but they have a profound influence on how children view their schooling, their own futures and the futures of their families. No longer are you able to point to the inevitability of 'a good job' if children work hard at school. This may seem to you to be an issue of little concern to small children; however, as viewers of the Channel 4 programme *Seven Up* and its sequels will know, children are already thinking of adulthood when they are very young. This is an issue you should reflect on, before discussing the work patterns of people present or past.

● There are subtle pressures on children related to the nature and status of their parents' work. I am reminded of the little girl who said her dad worked down the pit, because many of the other children's dads worked there, though her dad was really an accountant! In another class it may be the child whose dad works factory shifts who feels his or her family does not match the others. Your own attitudes, non-verbal behaviour and gestures are also important in affecting children's views. Try not to let them show!

● Some interesting statistics about the distribution of people in different occupations in Britain, both now and in the past, are brought together in *The Longman Handbook of Modern British History 1714–1987* by Chris Cook and John Stevenson.

People's work: from nomadic to pastoral life

In ancient times men and women lived on the food they could collect or hunt and kill. Then, many thousands of years ago, people realised that they could plant and grow seeds and that some animals could be penned and kept; this marked the beginning of a more settled life for people. Hoes and ploughs were invented, and thenceforward agricultural methods saw little change until the 18th century. Selective animal breeding, seed-drills and the rotation of crops were ideas introduced to increase yields. Modern farming is highly mechanised and scientific; far fewer people work the land nowadays.

Jobs for men in history

The story of men at work is predominantly one of a change, after hundreds, maybe thousands of years of work on the land and in home-based crafts to work in urban settings and on large-scale mechanised production.

The Industrial Revolution not only changed the location, nature and methods of work; it also eroded the autonomy of people in relation to their work. The machines needed no respite or change of pace and men and women were obliged to perform unstintingly, and for many hours at a stretch, as though they were part of the machines. In some respects this is still true today. Mills and factories drew in families who, because of enclosure acts, had lost their land and living. Men (and women) worked twelve hour days for six days a week. Cheap housing for these families was overcrowded and insanitary, and contributed to ill health. In addition to factory work there were other jobs essential to industrialisation. Men built canals, railways and roads, and they hued coal (women and children also worked in mines), often in frightful and dangerous conditions.

From the 1830s onwards working conditions gradually improved, and the establishment of trade unions meant that workers began to exert some influence over their working conditions and rates of pay. By 1990 there were 1300 unions with 2 million members. The Labour Party was founded in 1893.

During this century there was mass unemployment between the wars. Britain has had to face fierce competition from new industrial nations and increasingly automated production. This means there are fewer jobs than there used to be in some sectors.

In addition to those who worked and work the land and in factories, you may choose to study other occupations, like those of shopkeepers, soldiers and sailors. For the shopkeeper, the broad trend has been away from the individual craftsman or maker and seller of goods, to the mass production of items that are sold in multiple-chain stores. For soldiers, the Crimean War marks the point at which the 'profession' of soldier became established. Before that time men were pressed into service, often under false pretence. Conscription survived until 1960, so it is still in the memory of many older men that they gave part of their working lives to the national forces. For many years conditions for the average seaman were harsh and squalid, despite the enormous importance to British history of both fighting ships and merchant ships. In the early part of this century Britain depended on its shipping in many ways. For example, in 1939 half our food and most industrial raw materials came from abroad by ship. Steam power was superceded by petrol and diesel and the fuel was brought in by sea.

Jobs for women in history

At the time of the Norman Conquest women worked the land with their menfolk, and were also responsible for feeding and clothing the family. The cloth for this was produced at home, made from sheep's wool which had been washed, carded, spun and woven. Some of it may have been home-dyed using vegetable dyes. All this was women's work. In medieval times middle-class women became unofficial partners in their husbands' businesses, and women sometimes ran alehouses, cook-shops and bakehouses. After the dessimation of communities wrought by the Black Death in the 14th century the manorial system failed to revive and a new class of yeomen arose. Their women still helped in the fields during haymaking and harvest. They also produced eggs, butter and cheese to sell at market. Later on the enclosure acts and industrialisation affected women's work choices alongside those of the men.

In the twentieth century war changed the pattern of women's work, and society's attitudes to it. Women were required to work for the war effort and some took on jobs which they would not have been able to do in peacetime. Women's war work and suffrage (women were able to vote at 21 from 1928) have been two powerful factors that have affected the work choices available to women now.

Child labour

Children worked to help the family from the earliest times and this tradition continued well beyond the coming of the Industrial Revolution. Around the 1900s a quarter of all 5 to 13 year olds worked part-time and about half of those were aged 10 or more (at the age of 12 children could get official exemption from school to work part-time). In fact, many children as young as 12 or 13 worked well into the 1920s. Boys worked in factories and at ship-building, mining and other industries, while girls were mostly working in domestic service, factories and trades like dress-making. Children worked because the money was needed to feed and clothe the family. Latterly, gradual improvements in the general standards of living, reductions in family size and changing attitudes to childhood, along with legislation on education and rules of employment, have meant that few children work like this in Britain now.

RESOURCES ▶

Artefacts

Collect things people use now and have used in the course of their work in the past. For example, you may be able to obtain some of the following:

— a Davy lamp and miner's helmet;
— part of a policeman's or woman's uniform, including whistle and truncheon;
— a nurse's uniform;
— a vet's or doctor's coat, thermometer and stethoscope;
— tools commonly carried by a mechanic;
— a representative's or sales person's publicity material and order forms;
— a chef's hat, ladle, saucepan and some cooking implements from the past;
— a dancer's practice leotard.

Equipment used in offices in the past, including a ledger, quills, dip-in pens, inkwells and blotters would also be of interest.

Pictures and photographs

Include some of people at work now and in the past in a wide range of occupations, using as sources books, paintings and newspapers. Contemporary pictures of farms and factories and 'below stairs' photographs may be available from the library or the archives of the local newspaper.

Story books

The workplace is another aspect of life which does not seem to feature much in fiction for young children. Perhaps you will be able to rely on 'real-life' stories told by relatives of the children themselves. These few titles will give you a start.

Berenstain, S. and J. *The Berenstain Bears go to Work*, Collins.
Cunliffe, J. The *Postman Pat* books, Andre Deutsch/ Scholastic.
De Jong, E. *Aren't They Wonderful?* and *Isn't She Clever?*, Andre Deutsch.
Drummond, J. *Wallace's School Adventure*, The Amaising Publishing House.
Worthington, P. The *Teddy Bear* books (Boatman, Baker, Farmer, Coalman, Postman), Picture Puffins.

Information books

Civardi, A. *Things People Do*, Usborne.
Cooper, A. and Bentley, D. *Police Officer* from the series 'People Who Help Us', Wayland.
Corbridge, F. *The Ambulance Service* from the series '999', Wayland.
Simson, D. *Lorry Driver*, A & C Black.
Stewart, A. *The Nurse*, from the series 'Cherrystones', Hamish Hamilton.
Turner, D. *Victorian Factory Workers* from the series 'Beginning history', Wayland.

CORE ACTIVITIES

1 My dad's job

Talk to the children about what their dads do. If they are unemployed, talk about the sorts of jobs they like to do. With the children's help, sort these out; depending on the range of jobs mentioned, you may prefer to display them as sets or as a block-graph. Your discussion need not be limited to the names of jobs, you can ask the children to describe the kinds of things dad does when he is at work.

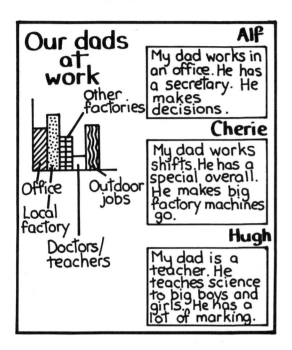

2 My mum's job

In a separate session from Activity 1, talk to the children about the jobs their mums do. Do not forget the work of the housewife! Display the results. You could then look at all the 'jobs' that mums and dads do that are not paid work, as well as the jobs that mums do for which they receive a wage.

3 What I want to be

Discuss the children's ambitions with them. Make a concertina book showing giant cut-out people to depict what the children would like to do when they grow up (see below).

4 Jobs of other people in my family

Ask the children about all the other grown-ups in their family. Perhaps they know about the jobs of their uncles and aunts, and their grandparents may be at work too. If you think it is appropriate, you could give the children a simple worksheet to complete at home, telling about the jobs of two grown-ups in the family other than their parents. Do let parents know in advance that you need the information because the children are looking at a variety of jobs that people do now and have done in the past.

Copymaster 51 is a data-collection sheet. If they like, the children can colour in the two outline figures at the top, representing the two people questioned.

5 Family work traditions

Are there jobs that are traditional within some of the families represented in your class? Your own enquiries and information from Activity 4 should show any patterns. If the patterns are marked, this is a perfect opportunity to mount a 'family' display showing several generations and highlighting the years spanned, the continuity and the changes.

6 Visitors

Ask community leaders and managers in local business whether there are people in various occupations who would be willing to talk to you about their jobs. After a preliminary interview, during which you can find out whether the person concerned would be

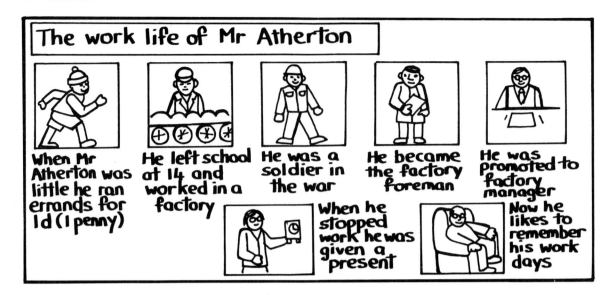

able to talk to children without patronising them, and whether he or she has interesting things to say about the past as well as the present, you can ask if they would be willing to come and talk to children in school. Some police authorities and fire services have people specially assigned to liaison with school-children. Prepare the children so that they know what they want to find out from their visitors, and (if the visitors are willing) tape-record the interviews. Ask the children to paint and draw people doing some aspect of their work and to add captions (see above).

7 Work on the land long ago
Choose a period of history and find out about how the land was worked. You may, for example, choose to look at medieval serfdom or the developments in mechanisation and crop rotation in the eighteenth century. Help the children to research and produce a frieze showing their findings in pictures, or make up a short drama related to the issues. This need not be an elaborate affair; the children do not even need to dress up. For example, suppose the setting is the eighteenth century; groups of children could represent the crop yields, the old-style farmers and the innovators.

8 Work on the land now
For comparison with Activity 7, discuss with the children the ways in which modern farming is carried out. Create a model farm and compare this with farms of long ago depicted in painting and photographs.

Copymaster 52 invites children to record three ways in which farming has changed over time.

9 Other outdoor jobs, past and present
Look with the children at a variety of other jobs traditionally done outdoors, both now and in the past. You could include, for example, delivery of the post, milk rounds, refuse collection and the police, as well as builders, roadworkers and those in the transport industry. A study of postmen draws in the history of the postal service; focus on the police opens up a discussion of the establishment of our police-force; and on builders a discussion about jobs which have sometimes superceded the work of craftsmen of the past (see Activity 10). Make folded card records depicting jobs in the past on the left and jobs in the present on the right.

10 Crafts of long ago
Use the school community as your starting point. If you work in a village there may be houses that are or once were thatched for you to look at and talk about. Perhaps the village once had a blacksmith and a cobbler. The oldest residents or local historians may be able to give you information about past craftsmen, which you can pass on to the children. If you work in town, you may still be able to trace the site of the local cobbler or tailor. Make sure that the children know what these people did, how they learned their crafts, and what may have caused the craft to die out.

Tell the story of Agnes, the maid at number 22. Her boyfriend is butler at number 28. The families they work for are very cross about this. Tell of the cross words that are said. What do you think happens to Agnes?

Copymaster 53 gives children the chance to write about or draw someone doing a craft of their choice and **Copymaster 54** depicts some people at craftwork, for the children to use as discussion pictures.

11 Factory work long ago

Talk to the children about factory conditions 150 years ago. Show them pictures of people at work in those times, and explain that it is humane laws that have changed people's working conditions. Look at pictures of modern factories and help the children to make some comparisons between the past and now. Display the pictures so as to invite further comparisons.

12 Domestic work

Find out whether any children in your class have a cleaning lady or *au pair,* or whether any of them have a relative who is a cleaning lady or *au pair!* Talk about the time (possibly before their grandparents were born) when many people had servants. Some children may know that their predecessors were servants. Tell the children that many households had more than one servant – in large households the housekeeper and butler were the most senior servants and they might have had several servants beneath them. Show the children photographs of Victorian and Edwardian servants, and explain that the life of a servant was often very hard work for very little reward.

On **Copymaster 55** children can write some of the reasons why they would not like to have been a servant long ago. **Copymaster 56** is a cut-away picture of a middle-class Victorian house at the turn of the century. The children can study the detail in the rooms and write about what went on in each. Point out the servants' sleeping quarters in the attics and their working area in the basement. The children could each make and colour a front for their house which could be attached at the side so that it opens. These houses would make an attractive frieze, and the starting point for stories (see above).

13 Changing office work

Assemble a collection of things that would have been found in an office in the past. Include an old ledger, some 'copper-plate' writing, quills, blotters and ink. Alongside, place an old typewriter (the older the better) or a page of typing, a telephone, a word processor or a word-processed passage, and details of telex and fax machines. Invite the children to comment on the ways in which work in an office has changed in the last one hundred years. (See below.)

14 The story of women at work

Collate all that the children have learned about the jobs of women now and in the past. Lay out all this information in chronological order and point out to the children that women now do a wider variety of jobs than they did long ago.

Office equipment

A quill-pen and handwritten record   A typewriter   A word processor with printout

FAX machines   Telex

Long ago ————————→ Now

EXTENSION ACTIVITIES

1 A look at an occupation in the past
Let the children choose an occupation and find out all they can about its history. For example, they may choose 'doctor' or 'explorer'. Their work could involve famous names if you wish.

2 A factory and museum visit
Visit a modern factory and a factory museum and compare the two in as many ways as possible. For example, ask the children about the amount of space for the workers, how the factory is or was heated and lit, and what the noise levels and standards of cleanliness are or were.

3 Teacher's shadow
Let the children shadow you for a day (if you can stand it) and record in words and pictures what you do. Then let them look at pictures and descriptions of classroom life in the past and see if they can tell the story of a day

in the life of a Victorian teacher. They can look for points of comparison. Discuss also which other jobs could be studied in this way, and what can be learned from watching people at work that cannot be learned 'at second hand'.

Topic: Going to work. Suggested level(s) of work involved in activities

Core Activity Number	Level	Core Activity Number	Level	Extension Activity Number	Level
1	1/2	8	2/3	1	3
2	1/2	9	3	2	3
3	1	10	3	3	3
4	2	11	3		
5	1/2	12	3		
6	1/2/3	13	2/3		
7	3	14	3		

PEOPLE AND ANIMALS

TOPIC WEB

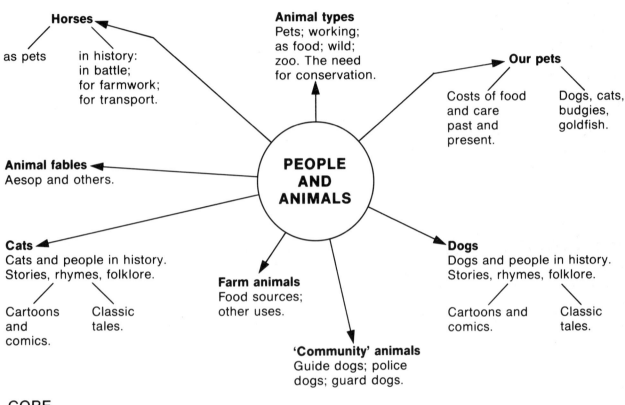

Horses

as pets

in history:
in battle;
for farmwork;
for transport.

Animal types
Pets; working;
as food; wild;
zoo. The need
for conservation.

Our pets

Costs of food
and care
past and
present.

Dogs, cats,
budgies,
goldfish.

Animal fables
Aesop and others.

PEOPLE AND ANIMALS

Cats
Cats and people in history.
Stories, rhymes, folklore.

Cartoons
and
comics.

Classic
tales.

Farm animals
Food sources;
other uses.

Dogs
Dogs and people in history.
Stories, rhymes, folklore.

Cartoons and
comics.

Classic
tales.

'Community' animals
Guide dogs; police
dogs; guard dogs.

CORE

EXTENSIONS

Animals of local interest
An aviary, zoopark,
pigeon club.

Animal symbols
Trademarks, logos and badges.
Advertising.
'Meanings' attributed to animals.
Heraldry.
Symbolism on tombs.

THIS TOPIC AND THE NATIONAL CURRICULUM ▶

Work in this topic can be treated as part of a broader cross-curriculum theme with links including the following:

English   All aspects
Mathematics   Animal facts, for example, speed, size,
   weight, wingspan
Science   All animal life
Technology   Making things from animal hides, wool
   and feathers and bone

Geography   The distribution of animals; threatened
   habitats
Creative arts
— *Art*   drawing and painting pets; designs using
   animal motifs
— *Drama*   animal-like movement in dance

ABOUT THIS TOPIC ▶

General points

● Incidents involving animals and people hit the headlines every day. Many people are notoriously sentimental about some animals, as wrangles about dogs that have harmed people show. Not everyone minds how animals are reared, nor are they concerned about whether animals are used in research experiments, but the treatment of pet animals seems to be an issue on which everyone has an opinion. Your role in doing this topic is not to influence children to become animal-rights activists, nor to be over-caring about some animals compared with people, nor to be indifferent to animals, but to understand that people and animals have co-existed for many thousands of years and that animals have at times proved indispensable to people. An appreciation of that alone will affect the children's treatment of animals and their views on domestic rearing and conservation. It may even help to modify the future of man and other animals.

● The focus in the activities is on some animals that are readily accessible and familiar to children. For the Extension Activities there are some suggestions which include investigation of more 'unusual' species.

People and animals in history

Dogs rate as the most popular pet in Britain now, and were the first species to be 'tamed'. For thousands of years dogs have acted as companions, guards, hunters and eventually helpers in herding other animals. It is thought that, because a dog is a pack animal and used to a leader, it may have been relatively easy to train dogs to regard a person as a substitute leader. Evidence of the earliest domestic dog found in Germany is thought to be 14 000 years old. Nowadays, dogs are not only kept for their ancient uses, but also as guides for the blind, 'hearing' dogs for the deaf, and to work in the police and other forces.

Cats have been kept as pets for about 5000 years, though some sources say the first unequivocal evidence dates from 1800 B.C. In ancient Egypt cats came to have a set of beliefs attached to them, culminating in deification. The cat goddess was called Basht. Pet cats were so revered that when they died they were honoured in the same ways as humans, and people shaved their eyebrows in mourning. For the Romans cats symbolised freedom, and they allowed them (but not dogs) into their temples. It was in Roman times that cats were introduced into Britain, perhaps primarily to keep grain stores rat-free. In A.D. 936 a law was passed making it illegal to kill cats. By the 1600s cats began to be associated with witches and 'bad luck', but they again became popular with the Victorians for whom they represented cleanliness and good motherhood.

Horses have a very important role in our history. Millions of years ago horses were hunted for food. Later in history they were made to pull carts and farm implements, and therefore were the mainstay of farming and transport methods. Oxen were often used in ancient times for they seemed to perform better than horses, though it may have been inappropriate harnesses which cut into the horses' windpipes that made them do less well. Horses carried men into battle until about a hundred years ago. Now they are mainly used for riding for fun and for racing, polo and other sports.

The list of 'traditional' farm animals in addition to horses includes, for example, cattle, goats, sheep, pigs, chickens, ducks and geese. The first three of these are 'multi-purpose' animals and have yielded meat, milk, and hide or wool. Goats are thought to have been domesticated before sheep (at least 9000 years ago). At about that time pigs came to be reared for their meat and skins, and their fat and bristles proved useful too. Despite their long history as domestic animals, chickens were more probably reared for sport (cock fighting) and meat than for eggs, which only began to be eaten in quantity after 1800. Chickens were domesticated about 6000 years ago; ducks and geese much more recently, about 500 B.C.!

The Protection of Animals Act of 1911 says it is a criminal offence to hurt an animal or abandon it or transport it in poor conditions. Subsequent laws have extended the 'rights' of animals still further.

RESOURCES ▶

Artefacts

Provide 'pet' equipment; a model farm and model farm animals; and old and modern comics depicting animals.

Information

This could consist of, for example, animated films concerning animals, and the history of the uses of guidedogs for the blind and police dogs and horses.

Paintings and sculpture

The possibilities are legion; here are a few suggestions to start with: reproductions of French cave-paintings, perhaps those from the Dordogne region; pictures of Egyptian and Roman statues and relief-work including animals; pictures of the Bayeux and other tapestries depicting animals; Tudor pets depicted in the painting entitled *The Tenth Baron Cobham and his Family* (shows a dog, guinea pig or hamster, a monkey, parrot and finch); paintings by Goya, Gainsborough and other portrait artists who included animals in their works; paintings of dogs and horses by Stubbs.

Story books

Traditional tales which feature animals, like *Jack and the Beanstalk, The Golden Goose, Puss in Boots, Dick Whittington* and *Alice in Wonderland* appear in a variety of editions and should be easy to find. In addition, there is an enormous range of stories, particularly about pets, and easy-to-read information books about their care. The historical information is, however, often too brief. Below are a few suggestions to set children going.

Allen, J. *My Dog,* Picturemac.
Bauer, S. *My Cat, Kipper,* Andersen Press.
Berg, L. *My Dog Sunday,* Young Puffin.
Campbell, R. *Dear Zoo,* Picture Puffin.
Drummond, J. *Wallace's School Adventure,* The Amaising Publishing House.
Haley, G. *The Post Office Cat,* Methuen.
Herriot, J. *Bonny's Big Day* and *Only One Woof* (and many others), Michael Joseph/Piccolo.
Kerr, J. The *Mog* books, Collins.
Kerven, R. *Legends of the Animal World,* Cambridge University Press.
King, D. *Rex QC,* Pavilion Books.
Le Guin, U. K. *A Visit from Dr Katz,* Collins.
Lewis, K. *Emma's Lamb,* Walker Books.
Lewis, T. *Oh! Pebble,* Macdonald.
Lingard, J. *Morag and the Lamb,* Walker Books.
Lobel, A. *Fables,* Jonathan Cape.
McClure, G. *Cat Flap,* Andre Deutsch.

McGovern, A. *Little Whale,* Scholastic.
Moore, I. *Six Dinner Sid,* Simon and Schuster.
Moray-Williams, U. *Gobbolino the Witch's Cat,* Harrap/Young Puffin.
Morpurgo, M. *Jigger's Day Off,* A & C Black.
Ormerod, J. *Kitten Day,* Walker Books.
Pooley, S. and Chappell, A. *An Outing for Oliver,* Blackie.
Smyth, G. *A Pet for Mrs Arbuckle,* Hamish Hamilton.
Stranger, J. *Marooned,* Kaye and Ward.
Todd, H. E. *The Sick Cow,* Picture Puffin.
Tyrrell, A. *Annie's Goose,* Hippo Scholastic.
Waddell, M. *We Love Them,* Walker Books.
Watson, C. *Animal Stories,* Usborne.
Wildsmith, B. *Hunter and his Dog,* Oxford University Press.
Zion, G. The *Harry* books, Picture Puffin.

Information books

Hart, A. *Dogs,* Franklin Watts.
Hearne, T. *Pets* from the series 'Spotter's Guides', Kingfisher Books.
Hill, R. *The Usborne First Book of Pets and Petcare.*
Palmer, J. *The Superbook of Dogs* and *The Superbook of Cats,* Kingfisher Kingpins.
Potter, T. *Sheep* from the series 'My world', Macmillan.
Quicke, K. *Let's Look at Horses* from the series 'Let's Look at', Wayland.
Spector, J. *Spotter's Guide to Horses and Ponies,* Usborne.
Sproule, A. and M. *Budgies,* and other books in the series 'Know your pet', Wayland.
The *Pet Care* series from Hodder and Stoughton.

CORE ACTIVITIES

C57 –61

1 Different kinds of animal

As a starter discussion, ask for the children's ideas about all the animals there are in the world. Ask them which animals are 'special' to people and why. They may mention that some animals make good pets; they may also agree that farm animals and 'working' animals are important. Using models including farm animals, pets and zoo animals, talk about the sets these can be placed in, particularly in relation to what they do for people (see below).

2 Our pets

This is a favourite activity to do with children, and is suggested here because it can form the 'backdrop' to what the children subsequently learn about pets of the past. Begin by making a count of the pets represented. This is a good opportunity to start a database. Let each child write about their own pet, the school pet, a friend's pet, or a pet they would like to have. If they need help in structuring the writing try giving them some key ideas, for example, looks, food, funny tricks,

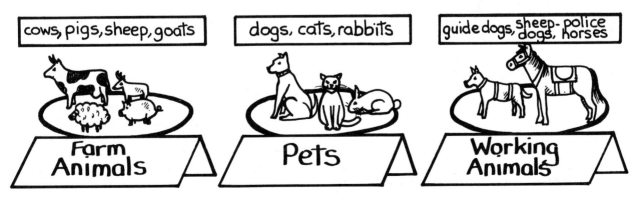

special place. Begin a display which will comprise information about pets present and past.

Copymaster 57 is a recording sheet for children to work on.

3 Dogs and people

Dogs have had a close relationship with people for so long that they were probably the earliest pet. With the children look for two sets of information. The first concerns all the ways in which dogs and people are known to have got along together, both now and in the past. Include here working dogs, like sheepdogs; hunting dogs; and police dogs and guard dogs, as well as dogs as companions. The second set of information is past evidence that dogs and people lived closely together, as demonstrated in pictures, paintings, drawings and photographs. Ancient relics like tombs, pottery and jewelry can yield evidence too. Let the children do a library search for pictures in art books and books about ancient civilisations. Add all the discoveries to the display, including, for example, copies and tracings of the 'library' pictures, those the children have drawn themselves, and clay models of sculptures. (See above.)

Copymaster 58 is a worksheet for recording facts about dogs in the past.

4 Cats and people

Cats have been kept by people mostly as pets, though a good mouser must have been an asset sometimes! The ancient Egyptians' attitudes to cats would be of interest to the children, as would a study of information and evidence similar to that used in Activity 3. Add all the children's work to the display or, if you have space, mount a display with one unit for gods and another for cats, and add to it as the children accumulated information about other animals.

Copymaster 59 gives the children a chance to record facts about cats in the past.

5 Stories, rhymes and folklore

Search for the appearance of dogs in classic and contemporary stories and rhymes, for example *One Hundred and One Dalmations*, *One man went to mow*,

How much is that doggy in the window? Compile a class book of these, along with children's drawings.

Tell the children about some 'classic cats'. For example, you could read passages from *Puss in Boots*, *Dick Whittington* and about the Cheshire Cat in *Alice in Wonderland*. Remind the children of the difference between fact and fiction – among these three only Dick Whittington existed (he may not have been as poor as the story says, but it is believed he had a cat). Poems that children enjoy include not only the traditional rhymes such as *I Love Little Pussy*, but also Lear's *The Owl and the Pussycat* and T. S. Eliot's *Old Possum's Book of Practical Cats*. Let the children paint and draw these cats and display the pictures with appropriate captions, alongside the books (see top of page 81).

6 Pet stories
Arrange a collection of stories about pet animals. Do a bit of research to find stories about pets in the past, both real and invented. For example, there is a tale that Dickens had a cat called William which had kittens and was promptly renamed Wilhelmina! Samuel Johnson had a cat called Hodge whom he fed on oysters! Give the children a chance to review story books, rank those they liked best, and say why they liked them. **Copymaster 60** invites the children to record their favourite pet story and also indicate what they have learned about people and pets.

7 Pet animals in cartoons and comics
Collect some comic stories depicting animals and their owners and list some cartoon animals. Talk to the children about how animals can be used in ridiculous situations to make us laugh, and some of the other reasons why so many cartoons have animals rather than people in them. Compare some vintage comics and cartoons with contemporary ones – Felix, Korky, Mickey Mouse, Tom and Jerry and Butch, Sylvester and Tweetie-pie will all be great talking points for the children.

8 Pet costs
The costs of keeping a pet nowadays can be high. Do the children know how much their pet costs? Discuss what people did to feed their pets before food could be bought from supermarkets in tins and packets. Collect some pet-food packaging, attach price labels to it and display it alongside pictures and models of the scraps and bones probably fed to dogs and cats long ago. The purpose of this activity is to use pet-feeding as an indication of our changing attitudes to our pets and our increased affluence, and to communicate the fact that prepared pet food represents a real addition to our family food budgets. In 1986, in the UK alone, £321 million was spent on canned dog-food and £329 million on canned cat-food!

9 Horses as pets
Nowadays horses are kept to ride for pleasure. If there are children in the class who go riding, they may like to do a piece of work or make a presentation to the other children about how they care for their 'pet'.

10 Horses in history
Help the children to show all that they know about the ways in which horses and people have related to each other in the past. Nowadays, horses in this country are chiefly ridden for fun and in sports, but they have a long history of helping on farms, acting as means of transport, and participating in battle. The dates for the commencement of these special roles are uncertain, but the children could still create a timeline. Perhaps they could show horses long ago pulling a cart or plough and being ridden into battle; then horses pulling canal boats and early buses; and horses nowadays racing and being ridden for pleasure.

Copymaster 61 provides pictures that could be used on a timeline and for a 'then and now' comparison. Top left is a scene depicting an eighteenth-century foxhunt and top right a dragoon from the time of the Crimean War. On the second row the pictures show a medieval joust and a hackney coach of the Stuart period. Below that is an ancient Bronze Age chariot with solid wheels, and one of the first horse-drawn buses from about 1830. Finally, on the bottom row, are pictures of modern children riding ponies for pleasure, and haymaking in the time of Elizabeth I.

11 Animals as food
Ask the children what is their favourite meat. Tell them that many hundreds of years ago people hunted and killed animals to eat. Then, over a long period, they learned how to pen animals and rear them near home so they no longer needed to hunt. Nowadays many animals are fed on exactly the right amount of pre-packed and measured food to make their meat good to eat. The animals are often kept indoors too, so that they can be protected from certain diseases and reared in 'controlled' conditions. List the animals kept in this way.

12 'Working' animals on the farm
Talk about cows and sheep which are not just reared for their meat. Discuss milk and wool production now and in the past. Include the contribution other animals make, for example, sheepdogs, and hens, ducks and geese that produce eggs.

13 Working animals in the community
Guidedogs for the blind and police dogs and horses may be the working animals that are most familiar to children. Ask the relevant authorities for some information about the history of these animals. Then help the children to dramatise one of the stories or put on a stick or glove-puppet show for their friends or a school assembly.

14 Animal fables and legends
Fables have a moral, while legends are frequently thought of as stories from the past that cannot be proved to be true. Begin with Aesop's fables like *The dog in the manger* and *The dog with the bone*. Discuss their meaning and the importance of stories like this to people both long ago and now.

EXTENSION ACTIVITIES

C62

1 Animals of local interest
Because of the location of your school, or a particular local interest, you may choose to look at some more 'unusual' species that have also had special relationships with people. For example, you may choose to look at birds because of a nearby private aviary or one that is open to the public, or a local pigeon club. Caged birds are still very popular pets and they have been kept for many thousands of years. Canaries at one time were 'working birds', used to test whether the air was fresh in mines. Hawks, too, have a history interwoven with that of man.

If the school is near a zoo or wildlife park, ask the education department there if a member of staff would be willing to talk to the children about people and animals and then take them on a guided tour.

2 Animal emblems
Look for trademarks, logos, badges and emblems that depict animals and, if possible, gather pictures of stylized animals used in traditional design. Discuss the use of animals in design and advertising, from the dog in the old 'His Master's Voice' ad. to the Dulux dog; and from the American eagle to the English bulldog. Let the children discuss why particular animals are chosen for design and advertising. What are the meanings and messages the animals convey? **Copymaster 62** allows children to draw some of the old and new animal emblems they find, and to make up some of their own.

3 Animals as symbols in heraldry and religion
This activity follows on from Extension Activity 2. Investigate which animals are used in heraldic devices, including lions, unicorns and deer, and what they mean in the various positions.

Look also for pictures of the stone effigies that are sometimes found on the top of old tombs. Some of these depict animals as well as the people buried in the tomb. Investigate the meaning attributed to the presence of the animal, for example a lion is said to denote strength, a serpent evil and a dog fidelity. If the children wish to pursue this activity further, you could investigate the use of animals as symbols in other religions and in ancient times.

Topic: People and animals. Suggested level(s) of work involved in activities

Core Activity Number	Level	Core Activity Number	Level	Extension Activity Number	Level
1	1	8	2/3	1	1/2/3
2	1/2	9	2/3	2	2/3
3	2/3	10	2/3	3	3
4	2/3	11	2/3		
5	1/2/3	12	1/2		
6	1/2/3	13	1/2/3		
7	1/2	14	1/2/3		

MONEY AND SHOPS

TOPIC WEB

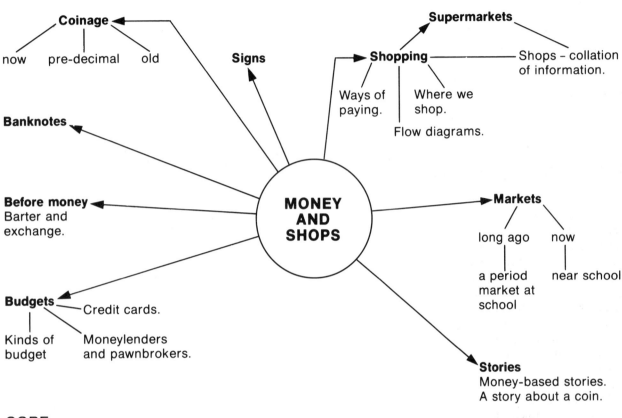

Coinage
now   pre-decimal   old

Signs

Supermarkets

Shopping
Shops – collation of information.

Ways of paying.   Where we shop.
Flow diagrams.

Banknotes

MONEY AND SHOPS

Before money
Barter and exchange.

Markets
long ago   now

a period market at school   near school

Budgets
Credit cards.

Kinds of budget   Moneylenders and pawnbrokers.

Stories
Money-based stories.
A story about a coin.

CORE

EXTENSIONS

Advertising
Press and other advertisements for shops, now and in the past.

Specialist markets
Local and national markets (e.g. Covent Garden).

Local shops
Now and in the past.

THIS TOPIC AND THE NATIONAL CURRICULUM ▶

Work in this topic can be treated as part of a broader cross-curriculum theme with links including the following:

English   All aspects
Mathematics   Play shop, shopping calculations
Science   How coins are made
Technology   Designs for coins and notes
Geography   Foreign currency and exchange rates, shopping on holiday

Creative arts
— *Art*   coin-rubbings, model shops
— *Drama*   re-enact the history of money, from barter to the credit card
Economic awareness   All the activities in this topic contribute to an understanding of economics

ABOUT THIS TOPIC ▶

General points

● Some families are more affluent than others, and you need to steer discussions about money and what we buy so that they do not become 'boasting matches' about wealth.

Money in history

For much of the history of mankind people have managed without money. However, barter does have one big disadvantage – you have to find someone who is willing to take what you have in exchange for something they have that you want. A 'medium of exchange', such as coinage, makes that direct mutual interest unnecessary. Before there was money, some societies used things like shells and beans, but a piece of metal as a token of exchange has advantages. If the metal is rare a small piece can be assigned great value, and it can be melted and made into different shapes. Also, it lasts, and it may not be heavy. From metal piece to distinctive coin with special markings is a small step. Nevertheless, even when coins had been in use for many hundreds of years, barter – or payment in kind – was still widely used, hence the tithe barns for storing peasants' dues to the church.

With the increase in the numbers of import and export merchants and the expansion of the shipping industry, shipping companies were formed, representing the shared 'investment' of individual merchants, who might see no return on that investment for some years.

The idea of a bank began among goldsmiths, who were then able to put gold left with them into a safe locked place. The goldsmith gave the owner of the gold a receipt so that he or she could reclaim it when it was required. If both the owner of the gold and the gold-smith were trustworthy, the receipt alone could be used to buy things. The Bank of England was established in 1694. Credit cards were invented in 1950. Decimal coinage was introduced in Britain on February 15, 1971.

Shops in history

Markets are places where people have come for hundreds of years to sell their own surplus goods and buy things they need. Even shopkeepers were often involved in producing what they sold until about 150 years ago. In many towns there were markets every week, and during the thirteenth century these totalled to around three thousand in England alone. All the goods sold had a tax on them that was paid to the town council. Anyone who was unfair in their dealings and was found out was punished severely, for example by being placed in the stocks or pillory. Large markets, held at infrequent intervals, were called fairs. As they were often held on feast days, you will find more information about them in the topic *Celebrations*. Travelling pedlars sometimes acted as middlemen between craftsmen and their customers, by carrying goods from one market to another. Buying and selling continued in this way until the nineteenth century.

Factories and railways greatly increased the output and distribution of some goods, and began the revolution in shopping habits and the availability of a wider range of products.

The first department store in Britain opened in 1863. Woolworth's and Marks and Spencer are important chain stores which began trading towards the end of the nineteenth century, but it is thought that Lipton's grocery shops were the first chain to be established in Britain, in 1876 in Glasgow. By the 1930s there were supermarkets in the USA, and the first covered shopping mall was built near Minneapolis in 1956.

RESOURCES ▶

Artefacts

Provide play-money; some British coins, including pre-decimal coins (kept safely in your bag); and a collection of foreign coins.

Information

Sources could include mail-order catalogues, advertising about sales and special offers in stores, and both recent and old editions of Kelly's Directory for the shops near school.

Photographs

Include some photographs of markets, shops, shop-keepers and people shopping, now and in the past.

Story books

Atherton, M. *Tom Goes Shopping*, Blackie.
Garland, S. *Going Shopping*, The Bodley Head.
Gordon, M. *Wilberforce Goes Shopping*, Kestrel Books.
Lobel, A. *On Market Street*, Ernest Benn.

Information books

Briers, A. *Money* in the series 'Topics', Wayland.
Steel, B. *Medieval Markets* in the series 'Beginning History', Wayland.

CORE ACTIVITIES

1 Shopping

The thought of going shopping can raise a groan amongst children. If that is the case in your classroom, find out why and use the reasons as a starting point for discussion about, for example, how some of us shop for all we need (clothes and food) nowadays, and tell the children that this was not always so. Ask the children what 'shopping' means, and with their help, write down the chain of events that enable shopping to take place. The exact components of this flow-diagram will depend on what is 'bought'. You may like to try to construct several diagrams, perhaps for a loaf of bread, a bunch of bananas and a pair of shoes (see foot of page).

Copymaster 63 provides an illustrated sheet on which the children can create a shopping flow-diagram.

2 Paying

Do the children know how things are paid for? Discuss the methods of payment and how money is used. Set right the views of children who think that banks give away money, or that everybody always has some! Make a wall-display, or act out a series of brief dramas in which a number of things are paid for, to illustrate different methods of payment; and ensure that these are explained. Include cash, tokens, vouchers, cheques and credit cards.

3 Our coinage

Look at the range of coins we use and then sort them and play games with them. Here are some suggestions for activities.

Let the children put them in order of size.
Let the children put them in order of value.
Make a 'feelie' bag, put a coin in and let a child feel and say which he or she thinks it is.

Play 'Which coin?' by saying, for example, that it has the Queen's head on the front and a rose and crown on the back.

Make a display with all the 'coin' games available for children to play. Do coin rubbings, find out what the words mean and record them on giant cut-out coins. The rubbings could also be grouped and stuck onto giant cut-outs of the appropriate coins, 'heads' on the front and 'tails' on the back.

4 Our banknotes

Let the children handle and look carefully at a five, ten and twenty-pound note. Tell them who appears on the front and back of each note and why. Let them see the watermarks. Discuss why notes have a number on them and what happens when we 'change' a note. Let the children find out whose face appeared on notes long ago (perhaps in 1940 or 1900).

5 Pre-decimal coins

Find some pre-decimal coins and tell the children about the change in our coinage in 1971.

6 Old coins

Look at coins even older than those in use at the time of decimalisation. Discuss their names with the children, for example, sovereign, guinea, crown, farthing. Make a reference book containing rubbings and stick-on coins, past and present, and photocopies of notes, explaining the words and pictures on them. Put this in the book corner.

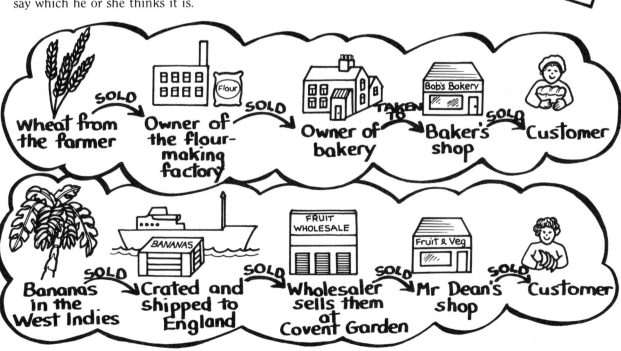

87

7 Before money

Tell the children about barter systems and act out bartering. See if the children can think of any advantages, and the disadvantages of this system of exchange. The latter include the fact that one transaction must meet the needs of both people or parties concerned. It does not matter how big your turnips are if all your neighbours have plenty, or if they can only give you wood (which you have in abundance) in return.

Copymaster 64 provides a picture story of a series of barters that the children can re-enact, retell orally, or put into writing.

8 Where we shop

Where do the children and their families go shopping? With the children's help, devise some questions which they can ask their parents about shopping now and when they were younger (see foot of page). Collate the replies and display them where the children can see them. **Copymaster 65** provides some starter questions to ask parents.

9 Markets long ago

Look for pictures of markets long ago. Let the children look carefully at these and spot clues as to where the markets were held, what was on sale, what sorts of people did the selling, and what the stalls looked like.

Copymaster 66 depicts a medieval market scene which can be used as the basis for discussion, and **Copymaster 67** invites children to draw some items for sale at a market in any period you choose. They can also draw the stallholder and what he or she hopes to take home instead of the goods sold. This might be money – or the stallholder might decide to spend some of his/her earnings while there is a good choice of things to buy.

10 Markets near school

If there is a local market, go along and check that it is suitable for the children to visit. Find a couple of stall-holders who are willing to answer a few questions put to them by children, for example, where they buy the goods they sell, whether they go to other markets, whether they also have a shop, and if the business has been in the family for more than one generation. Take the children along in small groups.

11 A school 'bring and buy'

With the help of willing colleagues in school and members of the PTA, arrange to hold a school 'market'. Each class could choose a different period in history, dress in the costume of the time, and fill their stall with things they have made that are 'in period'. For example, a medieval stall might have herbs, clay figures and woollen balls; a Tudor one might sell pomanders, lavender bags and stitched pictures; and a Victorian one might offer shell boxes, calendars made using sepia postcards, and greetings cards and tags using doilies and lace.

12 Money in stories

Find some classic stories the children will enjoy, in which money plays a central part in the plot. Dickens' *A Christmas Carol* is published in versions adapted for young children; Dick King-Smith's *The Queen's Nose* uses the idea of a magic coin; and, while money is not central to *Mary Poppins*, there are discussions involving David's wish to spend his money on food for the birds and his father's wish that he should invest it in the bank. Discuss the 'abuses' of money that result from overvaluing it.

13 Invent a story

Help the children to compile a group story in which a coin is lost in one century and is found again in another, and then goes through a series of 'exchanges'

Fleur and her mum go to the Sainsbury supermarket

When Fleur's mum Gaby was little she went to Mr Joe's shop

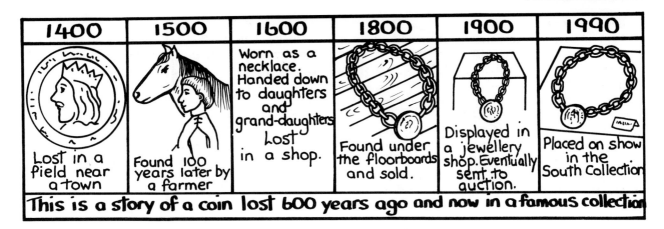

1400	1500	1600	1800	1900	1990
Lost in a field near a town	Found 100 years later by a farmer	Worn as a necklace. Handed down to daughters and grand-daughters Lost in a shop.	Found under the floorboards and sold.	Displayed in a jewellery shop. Eventually sent to auction.	Placed on show in the South Collection

This is a story of a coin lost 600 years ago and now in a famous collection

up to the present day. Explain to them that this 'story making' is not history, but that they can put into the story some facts they know about the past so that it will, in part, reflect what life was like then. Jill Paton Walsh's story *Lost and Found* uses the theme I have suggested here, and may prove useful to you and the children in working out how your own story line should go. Dramatise your completed story or put it into picture format with caption text (see above).

14 Shop and trade signs

When craftsmen set up in business in the past, a sign outside the building was their advertisement. These signs came to have easily recognised pictures on them. Find out what some old shop signs looked like and help the children to produce replicas, using printing, paints and 'junk' materials.

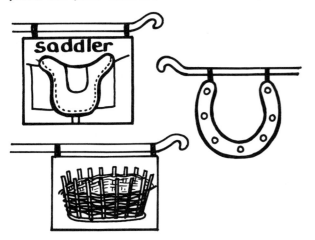

saddler

15 Budgets

Explain to the children what a budget is. Tell them that individual people, businesses, and families have budgets, but so too do whole countries. Explain also that the value of money rests in what it can be exchanged for. Long ago, some people earned only a few pounds in a whole year, but prices were much lower then and so they were able to buy food to last more than a few days! This is a difficult idea to get across to young children, who may have little direct experience of using money themselves. It is important however, because it illustrates the point that historians cannot look at one category of information from the past and make judgements from it about life at that time. The price of bread tells us little about people's standard of living, unless we also know their income, family size and expenditure on other things.

Talk to the children about the needs of a family for food, shelter, warmth, water and clothes. Devise some 'family' cards, each of which lists, on one half, the members of a family and what they need each week. These can, of course, be families from any period in history, but the data will need to be representative in terms of needs and costs. On the other half of the card show the prices of what the family needs. Give one card to a group of children, who can then work out what they can afford to buy with an income that you determine. To make the game easier, deal in whole pounds, or create an invented 'fun' currency for the children to use.

Copymaster 68 provides a sample card to start you off.

16 Moneylenders and pawnbrokers

Tell the children what these people do as a job, what the sign for a pawnbroker is, and why people use their services.

17 Credit cards

You may have talked about the use of credit cards when doing Activity 2. If not, explain to the children what they are and tell them that credit cards were not available long ago.

18 Shop–supermarket comparison

Assemble a collection of pictures of grocery shops long ago. Study these with the children and then compare them with modern supermarkets. Discuss the changes in shops which have occurred, for the most part within the children's grandparents' lifetimes.

Copymaster 69 presents pictures of a grocery shop before the First World War and a modern supermarket, so the children can mark and discuss the differences.

19 Shopping information centre

Make the play house into an information centre about shops and present all the information you have accrued about shopping. Stick posters and 'Did you know?' sheets to the walls and door. Word-process some writing the children have done and compile a 'shopping' pamphlet for each child, to which photo-copies of their pictures can be added. (See picture overleaf.)

EXTENSION ACTIVITIES

1 Shops in our town now and in the past

Choose a local row of shops. With the children, look at the current Kelly's Directory to see how they are listed. Search out and photocopy the appropriate pages from some old editions of the Directory and look at how the shops have remained the same or changed, both in ownership and in what they sell. Kelly's was established at least as early as 1878, so you may be able to determine which is the oldest shop in the area.

2 Press adverts for shops now and in the past

Look in local and national newspapers and magazines and on hoardings for shop advertisements. Find some from the past from old editions of newspapers and magazines and comment on the differences in presentation and selling points. Alongside some appropriate newspaper cuttings, display advertisements the children write themselves for imaginary shops selling anything from tricks, jokes and disguises to skateboards.

3 Specialist markets

If there is a suitable specialist market not far away, visit it with the children. Study one of the markets with a national reputation, for example, Smithfield or Covent Garden.

Topic: Money and shops. Suggested level(s) of work involved in activities

Core Activity Number	Level	Core Activity Number	Level	Extension Activity Number	Level
1	1/2	11	3	1	3
2	2	12	1/2/3	2	3
3	1/2	13	2/3	3	3
4	2/3	14	2/3		
5	2/3	15	2/3		
6	2/3	16	3		
7	1/2	17	3		
8	1/2	18	2/3		
9	2/3	19	2/3		
10	2/3				

CELEBRATIONS

TOPIC WEB

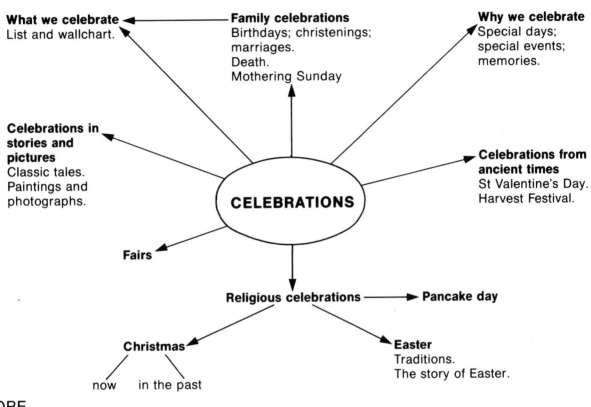

What we celebrate
List and wallchart.

Family celebrations
Birthdays; christenings;
marriages.
Death.
Mothering Sunday

Why we celebrate
Special days;
special events;
memories.

**Celebrations in
stories and
pictures**
Classic tales.
Paintings and
photographs.

CELEBRATIONS

**Celebrations from
ancient times**
St Valentine's Day.
Harvest Festival.

Fairs

Religious celebrations ⟶ **Pancake day**

Christmas
now   in the past

Easter
Traditions.
The story of Easter.

CORE

EXTENSIONS

**School
celebrations**
Logbook entries.
Major dates
in school year.

**Local
celebrations**
Origins and
how they are
celebrated.

Calendars
Investigate
special days
marked in
some diaries.

Rhymes
Research for
particular
celebrations.
Create a book.

THIS TOPIC AND THE NATIONAL CURRICULUM

Work in this topic can be treated as part of a broader cross-curriculum theme with links including the following:

English   All aspects
Mathematics   Calendars and dates
Science   Earth and space, taking photographs
Technology   Special recipes; card, costume and
decoration design
Geography   Traditions and celebrations in other
cultures

Creative arts
— *Art*   drawing and painting of, for example, gifts,
costumes, food
— *Drama*   re-enact a variety of celebrations from
different cultures, including nativity plays, egg-
rolling, May Day dancing

91

ABOUT THIS TOPIC

General points

● The children's experience must be the basis for your work in this topic. They may quite often attend galas, religious celebrations and big parties involving dozens of family members; or they may never have experienced a celebration of this kind. Thus the first activity aims to establish the extent of children's experience so that you can develop the topic from there.

● This topic is pre-eminently about continuity rather than change. Tradition, custom, and folklore are passed from generation to generation, often with little change over hundreds of years.

● Nations seem to accrue causes for celebration, not only through the wish to remember momentous historical events (for example, Guy Fawkes' night and Remembrance Sunday) and through traditional customs and religious beliefs (for example, Wakes Week and Christmas), but also with the accommodation of newly introduced religions and cultures. Thus Chinese New Year, Diwali, and Passover may be important celebrations in the calendars of children in your class.

● In generating a range of activities, the emphasis is placed on some celebrations that are and have been common in the British culture. You will need to choose those appropriate to the children you teach, and add additional ones that the children and their families can tell you about, and others that your own family celebrate.

● Some celebrations have mixed or uncertain origins, so sorting them is difficult. It may, however, be helpful to try grouping the kinds of celebrations you hope to cover. Here is one possible classification:

Ancient festivals   14 February (Valentine's Day), Harvest Festival, and 31 December (New Year's Eve) are well-known ones in this category.
Religious festivals   Easter and Christmas and festivals associated with other religions will feature here.
Our lives and families   Births, christenings, birthdays, coming of age, weddings, wedding anniversaries and deaths might be included here.
Events in history   5 November (Guy Fawkes) and 11 November (Armistice Day, the closest Sunday being Remembrance Sunday) fit in here.

● Be alert to the public concern about the exposure of children to pre-Christian beliefs. Your own lessons must be free of dogma or mention of any customs that may be disturbing to children. For example, Hallowe'en celebrations could be seen as undesirable for young children in a Christian society.

Celebrations in history

Markets are mentioned in the topic *Money and shops*. Markets were and are frequent and local affairs. In contrast, fairs were often held annually, usually after the harvest, and were large by comparison with markets. Fairs attracted entertainers – for example, bull and bear baiting, dog and cock fights, and fisticuffs sometimes took place there. Many people took away cheap keepsakes called 'fairings'. In

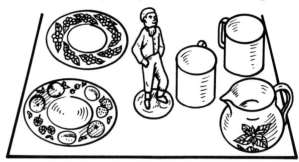

medieval times, many church feast days were celebrated with these fairs, giving rise to miracle plays and other traditions. 'Tollbooths' were usually set up to arbitrate where dealings were said to be unfair, and courts called 'pie powder' or wayfarers' courts (from the French *pieds poudres*, meaning 'dusty feet') were called to pass sentence.

Many ancient celebrations were carried on until well into Victorian times. Morris dancers performed at Whitsun, on May Day and during The Wakes; sword dancers at Christmas, Easter and on Plough Monday; and mummers at Christmas, Easter and on All Saints' Day. The mummers performed a traditional play about St George and a Turkish Knight but the underlying theme was the parable about growing corn.

Some examples of these ancient celebrations include the following:

— On May 1, the coming of spring was celebrated with dancing, a maypole, and a May-queen and parade. 'May birchers' left branches outside doors on April 30. Each tree had a different meaning for the people inside (for example, plum meant grumpy!).

— Some communities had men's (and occasionally women's) clubs which were formed to help in cases of sickness and unemployment. These held parades. With the introduction of National Insurance during this century, these groups have died out.

— The Wakes fell on the festival day of the saint in whose name the church was dedicated. They sometimes extended over several days and were times for family reunions and special food, and booths and stalls were set up to sell cakes, ribbons and trinkets. The Wakes began with a church service and rushes were carried in a parade to be strewn on the church floor, for the comfort of the congregation.

With increased urbanisation, improved communication and changing shopping habits, fairs gradually became less evident. They were still held in Victorian times for the sale of animals, wheat, cheese and cloth, and travelling entertainers continued to be a feature of them. Hiring fairs remained important to people in finding work and did not cease until about 1905.

RESOURCES

Artefacts

Provide reproductions of paintings, including, for example:

Breughel *A Country Wedding*.
Greuze *Village Bride*.
Steen *The Christening Feast, 1664*.

Story books

Heaslip, P. *Grandma's Favourite*, Methuen.
Lindall, F. *Emma's Surprise Birthday Outing*, Walker Books.
Lloyd, E. *Nini at the Carnival*, The Bodley Head.
Morris, N and T. *Carnival Time*, Hodder and Stoughton.
Pacholek, E. *Here Comes the Bride*, Andre Deutsch.
Pragoff, F. *The Birthday Party*, Dent.
Prater, J. *The Party*, The Bodley Head.
Simmons, P. *The Chocolate Wedding*, Jonathan Cape.
Smee, N. *The Invitation*, Collins.
Sowter, N. *Maisie Middleton at the Wedding*, Picture Lions
Thomas, I. *Janine and the Carnival*, Little Mammoth.

Information books

Arora, R. *Sikhism* in the series 'Religions of the World', Wayland.
Cooke, J. *Projects for Easter*, Wayland.
Hannigan, L. *Wedding* in the series 'Celebrations', Wayland.
Hannigan, L. and Nagrath, R. *Harvest Festival*, A & C Black.
Heaslip, P. C. *Grandma's Favourite*, Methuen.
May, R. *Hallowe'en* in the series 'Festivals', Wayland.
Mayled, J. *Commemorative Festivals* in the series 'Festivals' Wayland.
Mayled, J. *Feasting and Fasting* in the series 'Religious Topics', Wayland.
Miller, D. *Christmas Customs*, Ladybird.
Nottridge, R. *The Gunpowder Plot* in the series 'Beginning history', Wayland.
Pearson, N. F. *Stories of Special Days and Customs*, Ladybird.
Solomon, J. *Chopsticks and Chips* in the series 'The Way We Live', Hamish Hamilton.
Solomon, J. *Kate's Party*, Hamish Hamilton.
Thomson, R. *My Class at Harvest Festival* and *My Class at Diwali*, Franklin Watts.
Whitlock, R. *Harvest and Thanksgiving* in the series 'Festivals', Wayland.

CORE ACTIVITIES

C70
–72

1 Celebrations we remember

Talk with the children about what they and their families celebrate. They may mention, for example, birthdays, Christmas, homecomings, Guy Fawkes and Mothers' Day. The children's ideas should give you a 'master list' of celebrations for an annotated wallchart, including some of the words the children used in describing them. Not only will this provide a starter wordlist for the children, it will also be a reminder of the discussion and a spur to their thinking. You can decorate the chart with pictures from a few greetings cards which say, for example, 'On Your Wedding Day', 'Happy Birthday', 'It's a Boy!' and 'Happy New Year'.

Some of these celebrations could be the first ones the children work on, to find out how they started and how they have been celebrated over the years.

2 Why we have celebrations

Stick the 'Celebrations' list from Activity 1 up on the wall for all the children to see. Give them time to read it and then, in a later session, begin to ask why we have celebrations at all. Children may reply, 'Because it is fun', 'Because we want to mark the day as special', 'Because we want to remember', 'Because we want to

make memories'. This can lead the discussion into the kinds of celebrations we have. The children do not need to group or classify celebrations, but they do need to know that there are various sorts and something about their origins, history and established form. Add the results of this dicussion to the wallchart you have already started, with quotes from the children them-selves. Not only does this help them to associate the spoken word with 'on the record', it also means that you value what they say.

3 Celebrations from ancient times: St Valentine's Day
Discuss what people do on St Valentine's Day. Collect old valentines and look for pictures of Victorian valentines, some of which were very beautiful. Make some valentines using card, tissue and doilies or cut paper. Research what is known about the saint. Attach the pictures and the children's efforts to a section of a large display, to which you can add more information as the children do more activities.

4 Celebrations from ancient times: Harvest Festival
Discuss with the children how it must have felt in ancient times when crops failed or when there was a good harvest. What might happen if they only had food from a vegetable plot to last all the winter, and the weather or seed was so poor that the crop failed. Explain that long ago people had no artificial fertilizers to put on the ground, nor did they fully understand what determined the size of their harvest. Tell the children that Harvest Festival is a time to say 'thank you' to God for bringing the harvest in, and that people have celebrated this for thousands of years. If you do the activity in the autumn term, let the children make a special presentation of poems and writing about harvest time during the Harvest Festival assembly.

Copymaster 70 is for children to record the detail of how and why Harvest Festival is celebrated.

5 Fairs
Explain to the children that fairs were not like modern fairgrounds. Tell them about fairs long ago, including the facts that they were often held around feast days, and were like large markets where there was an opportunity for people to buy and sell, not only local goods but also things from other parts of England and even abroad. Describe how some fairs grew into events where there were entertainers, music, dancing and fun. Find out about some of the entertainments enjoyed and let the children do paintings to depict them.

6 Religious celebrations: Christmas now
Look at all the things we do which constitute part of Christmas celebrations. Include cards and gifts, decorations and trees, lights, carols and pantomimes, food, church services and visitors. Create a class book setting out all that the children and their families do at Christmas. Follow up with Activity 7, to present a picture of Christmas in the past.

Copymaster 71 depicts Christmas celebrations now and is intended to provoke discussion and comparison with the pictures on **Copymaster 72**. In discussion with the children, be sure that they understand that not all families can afford to celebrate Christmas like this. Be sensitive to the fact that there may be children in the class to whom this applies.

On **Copymaster 72** some of the most important aspects of a Victorian Christmas are illustrated. Victorian Christmas cards became more varied as the century progressed. On expensive cards silk, satin, plush and brocade were used as materials, together with lace and embroidery. Children and animals were the favourites for design, though landscapes, seascapes and floral patterns were also very popular. Religious subjects were much less evident than one might expect. Holly and mistletoe were used to decorate both rich and poor homes. Many cards showed children bringing home greenery for the festive season.

Before Christmas, ballad-mongers walked the streets, often with their families. They sang and sold Christmas carols. Life was very hard for the Victorian poor.

Attendance at church in one's best clothes was seen as an essential part of Christmas morning.

Christmas trees were decorated with candles, small presents, glass balls, paper lanterns and small models of toys and musical instruments. Tinsel and fairy lights are comparatively recent inventions.

Even in poorer households no expense was spared on the dinner. The 'plum pudding' was perhaps the central feature, decorated with holly and surrounded by blue flames burning in the spirit sauce. Early in the century, goose was the usual roast; it was only later that turkey began to be part of the menu – mainly in middle-class households.

Family entertainment consisted of story-telling, music, and games such as blindman's buff and charades. Snapdragon was a favourite – it involved picking currants out of a bowl of burning spirit and popping them into the mouth to put out the flames. Wealthier families would have employed a conjurer or someone to stage a magic-lantern show.

7 Religious celebrations: Christmas in history
Christmas trees were introduced as a custom by Prince Albert. Investigate the origins and development of all the other things we do at Christmas. For example,

Christmas wreaths and *Jingle Bells* came from the USA, and candles and liquor have their roots in Norse and Roman celebrations. These investigations could result in a stunning display; or you could make some card folders, in relevant shapes, to depict Christmas customs – one could be shaped like a wreath, another like a yule log. Let each working group in the class produce pictures, rhymes and writing about one or two customs (but not in the same session, for they will all need help with the research). Share the results with everybody.

Copymaster 72 illustrates a Victorian Christmas, which may serve as a starting point for discussion. (See the information given under Activity 6.)

8 Religious celebrations: Pancake day
Tell the children that Lent was a time of fasting for Christians. (Many children of other religions will understand about the idea of fasting.) For Christians long ago, the food forbidden in Lent had to be eaten up before the fasting started. Cooking pancakes was a way of using up flour, eggs and milk, but this pre-fast time was often an opportunity for carnival as well. For many people, pancakes are the only part of the tradition that remains, though there are local pancake races.

9 Religious celebrations: Easter
The story of Easter, which lies at the heart of Christianity and is a cause for celebration by Christians, demands faith for understanding. It is important to tell the story of what happened to Jesus, to explain that Easter is about new life and new beginnings, and that the decorated eggs and chocolate eggs we eat are symbols of that new life. Here are some traditional activities that you could do with the children:

Decorate some hard-boiled eggs using felt-tip pens.
Arrange a cardboard-egg hunt, with a small egg as a prize and a tiny egg for everyone else.
Make some hot-cross buns (though the tradition of these buns seems to have its origins in a pre-Christian custom).

10 Family celebrations: birthdays
Birthday parties may be familiar to everyone in the class. Discuss what we do to celebrate a birthday, and create a 'spread' by helping the children to make play-dough or junk-model food and displaying it with picnic plates on a cloth attached to the wall (see foot of page). Add some birthday photographs that the children bring to school to show, including past birthdays. See if the children can recount what happens on grown-ups' birthdays.

Mention the importance of a person's eighteenth birthday, marking the point at which he or she is considered to be a full adult and is able to vote and hold a driving licence. Explain that the age of being 'grown-up' has not always been eighteen.

11 Birth, christening, marriage and death
Talk to the children about how these events are marked in their families. Cover those celebrations with which they are familiar, and talk about the special things that happen to help people remember these times and act as reminders of the continuity of life.

12 Mothering Sunday
Find out what the children do on Mothers' Day and tell them that this celebration has a long history. In pre-Christian times people honoured the goddess Cybele, who was mother of the gods. In recent history, servants who worked away from home were allowed this day off to visit their mothers.

13 Stories about celebrations

Look for mentions of celebrations in classic texts. For example, there is the Cratchit family's Christmas in *A Christmas Carol*, and Philippa's birthday in *The Railway Children*. Read the relevant passages from these and other suitable stories to the children. Then let them comment on those clues that might indicate that the stories are set in the past, and discuss how the ways in which the events are celebrated differ from those they know today.

14 Celebrations in paintings

Show the children some reproductions of paintings depicting celebrations. Let them examine the pictures closely and comment on how the people seem to be feeling, what is going on, and whether the celebration is similar to one they have experienced.

EXTENSION ACTIVITIES

1 School celebrations

Using the relevant school logbook entries, help the children discover the key celebrations in the school calendar and record how the celebrations have gone over a number of years. Create a class book for the book corner, or start a database which can be added to year by year.

2 Local celebrations

Investigate something that is celebrated locally in a big way. If the school is closed in Wakes Week, or if there is a local well-dressing, an annual gala, fête or fair, let the children compile oral reports about the event, its origins, when it is celebrated and what happens. Send a compilation of the children's findings to the local newspaper, for printing amongst the coverage of the current year's celebration.

3 A celebratory calendar

Let the children consult a series of diaries (they need have no written entries), and record all the days marked as 'special'. For example, many diaries distinguish saints' days, Bank Holidays and religious festivals. Then ask the children to choose two of the days and find out all they can about them. **Copymaster 73** is a record sheet for a date chosen for investigation.

4 Songs, poems and customs

Write a list of about five major festival days that we celebrate. Let the children find a song, dance, rhyme or poem about each of them and write it in their own book of celebrations, along with details of when it was written and by whom. Teach the class some of the pieces and put the books in the book corner for all the children to consult.

Topic: Celebrations. Suggested level(s) of work involved in activities

Core Activity Number	Level	Core Activity Number	Level	Extension Activity Number	Level
1	1/2	8	1/2/3	1	3
2	2	9	1/2/3	2	3
3	1/2/3	10	1/2/3	3	2/3
4	1/2/3	11	1/2/3	4	2/3
5	2/3	12	1/2/3		
6	2/3	13	2/3		
7	2/3	14	3		

COUNTING AND MEASURING

TOPIC WEB

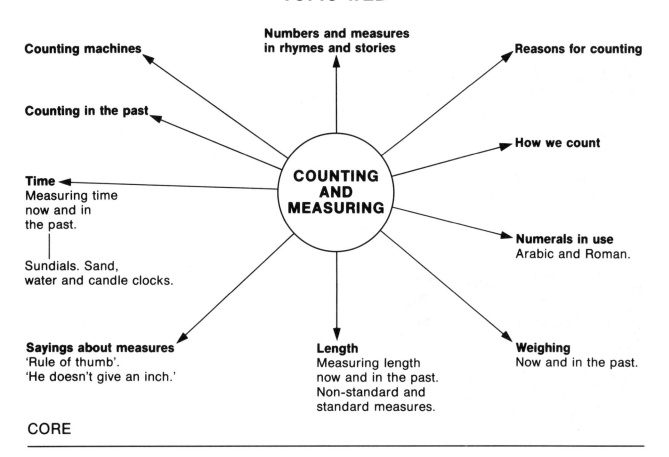

Counting machines

Numbers and measures in rhymes and stories

Reasons for counting

Counting in the past

How we count

Time
Measuring time
now and in
the past.

Sundials. Sand,
water and candle clocks.

COUNTING AND MEASURING

Numerals in use
Arabic and Roman.

Sayings about measures
'Rule of thumb'.
'He doesn't give an inch.'

Length
Measuring length
now and in the past.
Non-standard and
standard measures.

Weighing
Now and in the past.

CORE
_____

EXTENSIONS

A big clock
Investigating the
story of a familiar
'big clock'.

Instruments for measuring
For example, compasses
and weathervanes.

THIS TOPIC AND THE NATIONAL CURRICULUM ▶

Work in this topic can be treated as part of a broader cross-curriculum theme with links including the following:

English   All aspects

Mathematics ⎫
Science   ⎬ All the work covered in this topic
Technology ⎭ contributes to an understanding of
              the history of maths, science and
              technology

Geography   Location of ancient civilisations

Creative arts
— *Art*   patterns based on length, area, numerals and
  counts; models and constructions
— *Drama*   acting out counting and time rhymes and
  songs

ABOUT THIS TOPIC

General points

● This topic has been included because aspects of applied maths and science are important in everyday life, and they have a history just as do food or clothes or any of the other topics covered in this book.

● The topic is of central relevance to young children, who are just learning about our numbers system and measures. Confident historians can also become confident about maths, science and technology through work which some people might call history.

● Because the children are developing as mathematicians as well as historians, you may feel they display enough interest for you to investigate number systems other than those which are in common use in Britain today; that is, Arabic and Roman numbers.

● In the other topics in this book, I have advocated starting with the children's current experience and going into the past from there. In this topic, if the children are not skilled with numbers and standard measures, you may wish to begin with activities involving measures that are non-standard. This is frequently the order in which they are taught in maths, and it gives a rationale for the introduction of standard measures. The activities involving length and 'weight' are set out with the discussion of non-standard units first.

Counting in history

From the time of the beginning of mankind, people have needed to know how to share food equitably and how to make a simple count. When people started to lead more settled lives and first penned animals, it probably became important to be able to identify and count what they owned. It is thought that tallying may have been the earliest form of counting. Gradually number systems were developed – the Egyptian and Sumerian systems of written numbers are about 5000 years old. The idea of having a symbol for zero came from India, and this is essential to our number system today.

'Arithmetic' is a Greek word meaning 'to do with numbers'. The Romans based their number system on that of the Greeks, but after the collapse of the Roman civilisation it was mathematical discoveries in India that affected the progress of knowledge. In the middle-east, scholars studied the maths known from ancient times and it was from there that a knowledge of mathematics spread. By A.D. 1400, Arabic numerals were used in Britain, as too were the Arabic + and − signs.

Log tables were invented in 1614, the slide-rule in 1621, the computer in 1943, and the electronic calculator in 1971.

Measures in history

People in ancient times needed to know about the seasons so as to survive, and to regulate their activities. To judge when it was best to hunt and best to sleep, people looked at the sun and shadows. To measure longer periods of time than from sunrise to sunset, they may have looked at the stars. 'Sun clocks' or sundials, and candle and water clocks were early attempts to measure time.

In order to build structures that would stand, people needed to make judgements about measurement. These were often based on parts of the human body (hence, for example, cubit and foot). As people attempted more impressive buildings, standard measures were established.

When people paid dues in kind to the church, ways had to be devised to measure their payment by 'weight', and surveying was developed as a method of measuring the area of land involved. Eventually, money became the medium of exchange (see the topic *Money and shops*).

Geometry was developed through the public debates held amongst the early Greeks, the most famous of whom was Pythagoras. In about 300 B.C., Euclid wrote down all the complex rules devised to cover geometry. Since the discovery that the earth is a sphere, other geometries have been studied which take account of this.

Calculators and computers, electronic check-outs, library barcodes, digital watches, the speaking clock (started in 1936), time zones and stopwatches all enable us to do calculations and/or make decisions very quickly. Thus we can check, manipulate and control our own lives and surroundings in increasingly complex ways. Our number system and increasingly accurate and detailed measurement systems and devices continue to alter the course of our lives, and therefore our history.

RESOURCES

Artefacts

Collect things to use for making counts and for measuring, for example, counters, spent matches, number lines and abaci; clocks and watches, a sundial; yardsticks, metre-sticks, tapes and trundle-wheels; 'weights', a balance, and measuring jugs.

Pictures and photographs

Include pictures of clocks, rules and measuring tapes, balances, and weights and volume measures, all of which you will find in magazines, newspapers and catalogues. If possible, obtain pictures and photographs of these items as used in the past, as well as modern versions.

Story books

Hutchins, P. *Clocks and More Clocks*, Bodley Head/ Picture Puffin.

Walsh, J. P. *Lost and Found*, Andre Deutsch.

Information books

Catherall, E. *Investigating Numbers*, Wayland.

Williams, J. *Time* in the series 'Starting Technology', Wayland.

CORE ACTIVITIES

C74 –77

1 Why we count

Find out from the children what they know about the importance of counting. Establish with them these main points:

People have needed to count for thousands of years, in order that they may know whether all their animals and other goods are safe.

People need counts to assess 'fair shares'.

Numbers are important in communicating with other people.

2 Some ways of counting

Find out from the children the ways of counting that they know about. They may mention cardinal numbers (0, 1, 2, 3, 4, ...) and ordinal numbers (1st, 2nd, 3rd, 4th, ...). They may also offer 'ways', in the sense of devices, that help with counting, for example, fingers and toes, counters, spent matches, tallying, number lines and abaci. Experiment with all these methods of counting with the children, and display as many as possible on a table, where the children can continue to look and play with them when they have a moment.

You can extend the discussion for as long as the children continue to ask questions. How much they want to revise the idea of counts will depend on their skills in number, rather than as historians. The objective is to make sure the children understand that counts are vital, and have formed an important part of people's experience for many thousands of years.

3 Numerals we use and their origins

Show the children a sequence of our numerals, and the Arabic numerals from which they are derived.

0 – o		Y – 5
I – 1		⌐ – 6
ح – 2		7 – 7
۲ – 3		8 – 8
୪ – 4		9 – 9

Explain how the Roman number system works, and look for pictures which depict our use of Roman numerals today. You could include the numerals on clocks, watches and sundials; publication dates in some books; and page numbers on prefaces and newspaper supplements.

99

Roman numerals

I	1	VI	6	L	50
II	2	VII	7	C	100
III	3	VIII	8	D	500
IV	4	IX	9	M	1000
V	5	X	10		

Copymaster 74 invites the children to convert some numbers in their lives into Roman numerals. The answers are as follows:

Open-ended
12: XII
Open-ended
Open-ended
Open-ended (1992: MCMXCII)
The number of legs on a chair: IV
The number of faces on a cube: VI
24: XXIV   1672: MDCLXXII   606: DCVI;
73: LXXIII   58: LVIII   99:IC

If the children have a good grasp of place value, you can investigate the advantages of Arabic over Roman numerals for writing multi-digit numbers, which explains the widespread use of the Arabic system.

4 Counting machines

Get hold of several abaci or counting frames and let the children discover how they can help with counting. Explain that, for many hundreds of years, there were no machines to help with counting 'big' numbers. Look at several different calculators, and find a picture of an early calculator to show how cumbersome they were by comparison with modern ones. Discuss the point that calculators help us to compute far more quickly than most of us can do using pencil and paper, and also allow us to handle big numbers with ease.

5 Old words for counts

Find out about some of the old-fashioned words we use for counts. For example, we still buy eggs in dozens and half-dozens; a gross (144) may still be a way of buying nails; and paper is sometimes still sold in quires and reams. Ask the children to find out if their parents use any more of these 'old' words in the course of their work.

6 Measuring time now

Assemble a collection of pictures of the timekeeping devices we use nowadays, from the watches worn on the wrist by executives and divers, to those attached to waistcoats and nurse's uniforms; and from mantel clocks, and those which appear on the television screen during breakfast shows, to big clocks on top of buildings. Discuss the various faces, hands and numerals, and the distinctive appearance of digital watches and clocks. Explain that some clocks are powered by 'clockwork' (the energy is stored in a coiled spring), and others by electricity in a battery. Talk about the units of time we use.

Copymaster 75 presents pictures of actual clocks which can be used as the basis of discussion or put on a timeline. Top left is a modern digital wristwatch; then a British Rail Victorian clock (note that the 4 is written as IIII to avoid confusion with VI for 6). Next to that is an elaborate French rococo clock dating from the mid-eighteenth century. It would have had a hand-painted case and enamel dial.

The earliest evidence of the sandglass as a timepiece dates from around 1330. The most accurate of these were not filled with sand, but with finely powdered eggshell. The one shown top right is from the early eighteenth century.

The longcase clock on the left is typical of the early eighteenth century (about 1710); and below the BR clock is an early wristwatch. The first wristwatches were miniature keyless winding pocket-watches fastened to wrist straps; the one shown dates from around 1914.

To the right of that, above, is a mass-produced clock from the mid-eighteenth century; and below is a modern alarm clock for a child. The large street clock on the far right is French, from the late eighteenth century. By a system of pneumatic pipes it was operated by pulses of air from a master clock.

On the bottom row, centre left, is a bracket clock as made by Thomas Tompion (1639–1713), which has a mock pendulum. It would have struck the hours and quarters. Centre right is a modern digital clock.

7 Sundials

Describe how a sundial works and go and look at some in gardens, parks, or a garden centre. Find pictures of sundials which belonged to important people in the past, or have a special story attached to them.

Make a sundial (there are instructions in *Blueprints: Science 7–11*, Teacher's Resource Book, by Wendy and David Clemson, also published by Stanley Thornes). Compare times as read on the homemade sundial with the time on a watch. Discuss the disadvantages of using a sundial (the most important being that you only know the time when the sun is out!). Talk about the implications of these disadvantages for people living long ago.

Copymaster 76 gives children the opportunity to record their findings about sundials. The picture at the bottom of this sheet, on the left, shows one of the obelisks that the Roman emperors took from Egypt to set up in Italy. The surrounding pavement was marked out into 'hours' and an official was detailed to call out the time.

8 Sand, water and candle clocks

Long ago, people used the sun to measure time, but they also made other kinds of clocks. Find out about some of these and try making them in the classroom. Compare their accuracy with clocks as we know them, and discuss what this may have meant for the daily routines of people in the past.

9 Clocks in museums

A visit to see a collection of clocks is not one I would recommend in general for infants. However, if the school is near one of the places mentioned below, you could make a preliminary visit and see if a morning spent there would help the children's understanding.

There are over 100 museums boasting horology as one of the things they cover. Two important ones are:

The Science Museum in London, where the focus is on the technology of timekeeping.

The Museum of the History of Science in Oxford, which has a collection of astrolabes and sundials.

You could write to any museum which has clocks in its possession and ask for publicity material, out-of-date posters, and a catalogue of booklets and postcards your school might buy. These would help to resource a topic which feeds not only into history, but also into maths, science and technology.

10 Measuring length in the past

Tell the children that there was a time thousands of years ago when there were no standard measures. Before the age of standard measures, people are thought to have used 'parts' of themselves to measure. For example, you could describe a handspan, cubit, foot, pace and stride. Let a number of children try out these measures for the same tasks, and then discuss why their results vary. With the help of the children, invent a short story about a situation that arises because different people's measures vary widely because their bodies are different sizes. This could be re-enacted as part of a presentation or assembly.

Copymaster 77 is a record sheet for aspects of measurement using non-standard units.

11 Measuring length and distance now

Talk about the standard measures we use today. The children will need to know, not only about kilometres, metres and centimetres, but also about miles, yards and inches. Show them the speedometer on a car dashboard (marked in mph and kph). Show them also a pedometer, if you have one available. Look at some local road signs and signposts, or pictures of these, to find out how the distances are shown. Talk about the means available for measuring length, including rules, tapes and trundle-wheels, and let the children practise using these.

12 Weighing past

The need for standard measures in weighing and to calculate volume should be easy for the children to understand, after they have had some experience using arbitrary units like balls of Plasticine and jugs and beakers of various sizes. Discuss some old-fashioned terms, including a bushel, a pint (of prawns!), a pinch, a tablespoon and a cup.

13 'Weights and measures'

Find out what the children know about the units used in 'weight' and volume. Look at a collection of packs, cartons, tins and bottles to find out how these units are written down. Show the children that we use kilo-grammes and grammes, litres and millilitres, but that we also talk about a pound of apples and a pint of milk. Look at a set of 'weights' and some kitchen measuring jugs. Let the children handle and use these, and make estimates before trying tasks.

14 Everyday sayings

Investigate some of the things we say everyday that have their origins in number or measures. Here are some examples:

Rule of thumb.
It's as broad as it is long.
He doesn't give an inch.
Give an inch and they'll take a yard.
I'd go to any length . . .

15 Numbers and measures in rhymes and stories

Many children's playground and skipping rhymes involve numbers. See how many the children can collect, and then try to discover how old they are. Here are some examples:

One, two, three, four, five,
Once I caught a fish alive . . .

Ten little Indians . . .

Half a pound of tuppenny rice . . .

Sing a song of sixpence . . .

Folktales often contain references to numbers of things, too, and the children may like to think about how many stories seem to have special numbers attached to them. For example, there are three wishes, seven dwarfs, five beans and one hundred years.

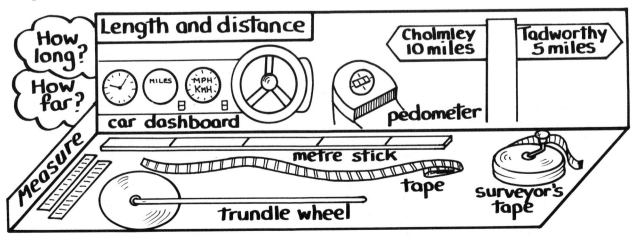

EXTENSION ACTIVITIES

1 A big clock

If the school is near a large church, a cathedral or a building with a big clock on it, help the children to find out the story of the clock. For example, they could discover how old it is, for how long it runs without maintenance, what powers it, what it is made of, and who made it. If it is a chiming clock, they can find out how that works too.

Copymaster 78 is a record sheet about a big clock.

2 Investigating instruments

Let the children follow their own interest, or assign each pair of children the task of finding out all they can about an instrument used for measuring. For example, a compass or windvane may lead into discovery about exploration and the development of ways of charting the weather.

Topic: Counting and measuring. Suggested level(s) of work involved in activities

Core Activity Number	Level	Core Activity Number	Level	Extension Activity Number	Level
1	1/2	9	3	1	2/3
2	1/2	10	2/3	2	3
3	3	11	2/3		
4	3	12	1/2/3		
5	3	13	2/3		
6	3	14	3		
7	3	15	2/3		
8	2/3				

SELF-APPRAISAL SHEET ▶

Name _____

When you can do a thing, tick the box.
Then take this sheet to your teacher.

Teacher's initials

I can set myself a question to answer about the past.		
I can draw an idea web.		
I can observe well.		
I can give an opinion and listen to others.		
I can think of questions to ask about the past.		
I can write down questions to ask about the past.		
I can find clues about the past in pictures.		
I know what the parts of a book are.		
I can find a history book I want in the library.		
I can get information from a database.		
I can put information in a database.		
I can find important clues in pictures and say why I think they are important.		
I can find important clues in stories and say why I think they are important.		
I can talk about differences between two reports about the same thing.		
I can tell other people about my discoveries.		
I can draw things from the past to show what they looked like.		
I can write in a way that is best for what I want to say (diary, story, poem, report).		
I can do research on my own.		

SUMMARY SHEET

Name of child/teacher(s) _____

Date _____	Date _____
Topic _____	Topic _____
Comments	Comments
Level	Level
Date _____	Date _____
Topic _____	Topic _____
Comments	Comments
Level	Level